RAMEN COOKBOOK

80 Step-By-Step Classic, Vegetarian & Vegan Recipes to Make Ramen at Home

Haru Okamoto

Attributions:

Vector images by Vecteezy.com

Table of Contents

Introduction

Ramen is perhaps the first thing that springs to mind when one thinks about Japanese cuisine. Because of its thick broth and excellent hand-made noodles, everybody is acquainted with this popular noodle dish. On the other hand, Ramen hasn't always been the Japanese delicacy that it is now.

Simply described, Ramen is a noodle soup made with a flavorful broth, one of many varieties of noodles, and a choice of meats or veggies, usually topped with a cooked egg. Ramen is considered a quick dish in Japan, with numerous tiny restaurants and street sellers selling this tasty soup. Although all ramen varieties are centered on the same idea; broth and noodle premise, the meal is extensively regionalized, with distinct versions served in different parts of Japan.

Ramen comes in various flavors, depending on the soup used, the noodles, and the toppings. However, the basic procedures for creating Ramen may be applied to any variation. To prepare Ramen, one must first prepare a broth. After you've settled on a soup, it's time to think about the toppings. A list of famous toppings, including Tamago & Chashu, maybe egg can be used.

All that's left are the classic ramen noodles after you've decided on the broth and toppings. These come in a variety of shapes & sizes and are used to make ramen soup. Tonkatsu is the most pleasing way to get started with Ramen if you've never tried it before.

Making a genuinely authentic cup of Ramen on your own is pretty easy & delicious & this book will assist you in doing so.

Chapter 1: Ramen & Its History

Ramen is usually regarded as a Japanese creation. However, whether the noodles were initially created in Japan or China, is a point of contention! It's easy to understand how the dish's roots may have become a little hazy: ramen-noodle restaurants initially became popular in both nations in the early 1900s, but noodles were referred to as "Chinese soba" noodles in Japan until the 1950s. The wheat noodles were likely officially created in Japan by Chinese laborers serving meals from food vendors, but Ramen's reputation in Japan exploded during the 2nd Sino-Japanese war, as Japanese forces came home from China with a newfound respect for Chinese cuisine. This resulted in an influx of new Chinese eateries around the nation.

So, although it's difficult to tell for sure, it's likely not too far-fetched to argue that ramen was originated in China and popularized in Japan. And there's no denying that, since its introduction, Japanese eateries have rendered the dish as their own. A substantial number of overseas Chinese have settled in the three main ports of Nagasaki,

Kobe & Yokohama, developing Chinatown, which offers a low-cost and rapid option for the impoverished working class. The wheat noodles were most likely brought to the Japanese by Chinese laborers serving meals from food carts.

It is reported that the Japanese nicknamed it "Dragon Noodle" at the time, implying that the dragon ate the noodles.

The name Ramen was coined during the Taisho period. Yokohama was reported to have made the first sighting in 1918. The first thing that comes to mind when thinking about Ramen in Tokyo. 43 years in the Meiji, the Lai Lai was the first ramen eatery in Tokyo. This shop has begun serving a Tokyo-style low-sodium soy sauce-based ramen made with kelp broth & bonito with chicken or pig bone soup.

Ramen has become increasingly expensive and challenging to come by over time. It has become a famous and very well gourmet meal due to the Japanese's ongoing exploration and re-creation. According to legend, ramen houses began to spring up throughout Japan in the 1990s, swiftly becoming must-visit sites for commuters and travelers. While it's impossible to tell for sure, it's certainly not too far-fetched to assume that ramen originated in China and was popularized in Japan. And there's no denying that, since its introduction, Japanese eateries have branded the dish their own. Ramen is now obviously a worldwide cuisine with fans from all over the world. The Ramen was not only kept on by the Japanese, but it also had an international impact.

1.1 Ramen's Origins and History in Japan

Noodles come in various shapes, styles, and sizes, and they all have cultural importance.

The noodle has spread throughout many continents and nations, creating deep roots in many civilizations, including cultural traditions in China like the Long Life Noodle to historic allusions in Tuscany such as the Regine pasta. Without question, the noodle has established close ties with Japan's history and culture. A special kind of noodle meal, Ramen, may be used to examine one relationship. Whenever one thinks about Ramen, one cannot help but link it with Japan. Ramen has become the most closely associated with Japanese culture. Ramen has a lengthy history in Japan, evolving together with the nation's state.

To start with, the origin of the original Ramen is uncertain; however, it is known that A Chinese immigrant meal inspired Ramen. The origins of Ramen and its subsequent rise are shrouded in mythology and mystery. There are 3 ramen origin stories, all of which are debated.

The original legend credits Shu Shunsui, a Chinese scholar, with bringing the ramen formula to Japan. Shu Shunsui was a Chinese government refugee who became a counselor to a Japanese feudal lord, Tokugawa Mitsukuni. According to historical sources, Shu Shunsui advised Mitsukini on improving the flavor of his udon soup. This meal is said to be the first Ramen ever cooked, making Tokugawa the first person in Japan to taste Ramen. Although Chinese culture indeed had a significant effect on Japanese society at the time, there is no historical document of Mitsukini preparing Ramen.

The following legend links the birth of Ramen to Japan's exposure of its ports to the rest of the globe. Chinese tourists were drawn to Japan's ports, and a Chinese noodle soup known as laa-mein was introduced. While laa-mein did not have any condiments and was not a dish in itself, much like contemporary Ramen, it is said to be a possible forerunner of Ramen today.

The most credible explanation links the origins of Ramen to a restaurant named Rai Rai Ken in Tokyo in the early 1900s. Rai Rai Ken hired Chinese laborers and offered Shina Soba, a noodle dish. Shina Soba combined elements similar to those found in modern Ramen, including pork belly, fish cake, and nori seaweed, into a single meal. During this time, Japan had become more industrialized and urbanized. Japan's industrialization and urbanization aided the popularity of Ramen. Shina soba was inexpensive and substantial, giving Japanese city dwellers plenty of calories.

Furthermore, mechanized noodle-making machines were widely used at the time. Thanks to these devices, the time it took to make the noodles were cut in half. All of these factors combined make Ramen the ideal cuisine to consume. It was the perfect meal at the perfect moment. Ramen became ingrained in contemporary Japanese urban life, establishing its first profound cultural and historical foundations in Japan.

Despite its strong roots in urban life throughout the 1900s, Ramen almost vanished during WWII. During World War II, rationing in Japan prohibited the consumption or sale of Ramen since it was considered a luxury item to dine out. Due to lack of food and mass starvation, the government imposed strict controls on food supply, and profits from the sale of food were outlawed. It was one of Japan's deadliest periods of starvation in its history, and it was still prohibited. Black-market food booths sprang up inevitably after the war ended. This was owing to the United States' continuation of food restrictions in Japan throughout their occupation. Unemployed restaurateurs who attempted to sell Ramen faced the possibility of going to prison-- and many did. During this period of famine and hardship, Ramen evolved to symbolize the polar opposite of what it does now. It was seen as a sign of a moment of need and the most fundamental of human needs. Luxurious meals, like Ramen, were out of reach.

Japan had a flourishing economic boom after World War II. The rebirth of the Ramen was aided by this time of substantial economic expansion and progress. Numerous building projects necessitated the hiring of a large number of construction employees. Ramen bowls were devoured in significant amounts by construction workers. Ramen had a variety of nutritious components that would supply enough energy to keep the employees well nourished and energetic. In Japan, several eateries that solely served Ramen grew more popular. Ramen was reintroduced as a traditional dish in Japan, which has seen fast growth.

Ramen's relationship with the after-war economic boom contributed to the "nationalization phase." Ramen had become more associated with Japanese culture as sellers went out of the trade, and broad Chinese stores that had launched Ramen gave rise to newer, more expensive eateries focusing on Ramen alone. Ramen became a national dish compared to the European cuisine that flooded into a newly prosperous country. It became an expression of nostalgia for a period when Japan was on the ascent rather than settled into wealth, thanks to its association with metropolitan workers.

Enter ramen tours, a craze that originated in 1982 in Kitakata, a tiny town in Japan. And there's Yokohama's Ramen Museum, which has been a million-dollar undertaking for the last two decades. And there's even an Instant Ramen Museum, called after its founder to mention the restaurant that helped popularise Ramen in the United States.

In addition, after World War II, a new kind of Ramen arose. Momofuku Ando examined the war's devastating consequences. Many people were hungry, and he judged that it was the most severe problem in Japan. He was motivated to develop a cuisine that would put an end to hunger in his homeland. He set out to create a non-perishable cuisine, inexpensive, quick, and simple to prepare. Ando wanted to develop his own Ramen after seeing how successful it had been in the past. Instant Ramen was the ultimate result! Quick Ramen was a hit because it allowed people to eat tasty Ramen in the comfort of their own homes at a low cost. Ando has set his sights on ending hunger with Ramen.

Ramen is now regarded as a symbolic and significant figure in Japanese history and culture. Ramen has grown in popularity all across the globe. Authentic Ramen remains an essential part of Japanese culture, although more ramen businesses have developed in major US cities. Authentic Japanese Ramen is still challenging to come by unless one lives in one of the country's major cities. On the other hand, instant noodles are now accessible practically everywhere in the globe. They're available at practically every grocery. Instant noodles are prevalent among students since they are inexpensive and easy to get. Even though Ramen has become a worldwide phenomenon, its deep roots will always be linked to Japan's past. Ramen has evolved into what it is now due to historical events in Japan and the individuals they influenced.

1.2 From a Handcrafted Dish to a Ready-To-Eat Noodle

The quick noodles developed by conventional noodles, according to history, address the features of hunger in a timely fashion. Taiwanese Ando Baifu's quick noodle is a game-changing innovation in the noodle world. Ando Baifu opted to remain a monarch after the war and contribute to the growth of Japan. He pondered how to create simple Ramen to keep and consume right away in his own garden. Later, the moisture in the noodles is removed by frying, making it difficult for them to rot. When you add hot water to the noodles, the water passes through the tiny pores in the noodles, softening the dry noodles.

Ando Baifu transforms the way people eat by speeding up the meal. According to some research figures, the world sells 1 billion packages of instant noodles each year, which is quicker and more profitable than McDonald's.

Chapter 2: Pantry Essentials to Make Ramen at Home

Flashy design, neon signage, and ridiculous furnishings are seldom seen in ramen restaurants. The majority of restaurants are simple—a few seats, one open kitchen where one can sit & watch your meal being produced, and often monochromatic walls. This is in sharp contrast to the bulk of contemporary dining establishments, which have interiors that beg to be photographed.

The dinner in Japan is the complete eating experience—and it's a fantastic one at that. Perhaps it's due to their passion for culinary art and meticulous attention to detail when it comes to every component. In any case, it's a tactic that works, and it tries to attract audiences. Local ramen eateries don't feel the need to make a lot of noise, especially online. You won't find famous influencers or complex marketing initiatives on Ichiran Japan's page—just Ramen, plain & straightforward

2.1 Minimalism & Japan

Marie Kondo, the decluttering queen, knows how vital simplicity is in Japanese society. However, the Japanese have been practicing simplicity for years. If you've ever questioned why zen gardens are so peaceful, it's because they were designed to remove distractions and provide space for thought and introspection. It's safe to argue that the same strategy has been used in ramen restaurants as well—even if all you're thinking about is how delicious a meal is.

2.2 Essential Ingredients for Home-Cooked Ramen

For homemade Ramen, you'll need the following items.

The most crucial advice is not to be frightened to try new things. Not locating the correct ingredient—or not like anything in a traditional recipe and replacing something else—has resulted in some of my finest innovations and discoveries. Recipes are only suggestions; feel free to add or subtract whatever you like. Don't like kale? Instead, why not try bok choi?

Noodles ramen

Ramen Noodles, Of course, the noodles themselves are one of the most significant elements. Even at Asian stores, you can have trouble finding the correct noodles. With the popularity of ramen bars, bundles of noodles are becoming more convenient.

The vacuum-packed individually wrapped fresh noodles are commonly available at Asian stores beside the dried noodles. In Asian stores, you may get both dry and fresh, refrigerated noodles.

If you can't locate them, try Sharwood's Medium Soft Noodles, which are just repackaged vacuum-packed ramen noodles. The most evident of all the ingredients. It makes no difference whether you buy the fresh or dried versions. They work great in ramen soup in any case. Depending on the brand, some ramen noodles have no added artificial colors or preservatives.

Stocks

If you want to make authentic Ramen, start by preparing a stock, usually made from pig or chicken bones or a combination of the two. But the procedure is quite time-consuming, even when using a pressure cooker. When it comes to cooking ramen soup, you certainly need a foundation. And the base in issue is dashi, a sort of basic stock often used in Japanese cuisine. Indeed, you may use regular chicken or veggie stock. However, if your goal is to produce the most genuine ramen soup possible, it would negate the point. Kombu & Bonito Flakes are essential ramen ingredients.

Rather than spending all day in a hot kitchen slaving over a stockpot, you can purchase high-quality stock sachets from the store. Some people will be offended by this since a lot of the richness in Ramen comes from the base's intensity; you can always prepare from scratch, which is more advisable.

Dashi Stock

This stock is prepared using bonito flakes (that is, dried tuna), which smells like fermented fish in the kitchen. Waitrose sells ready-made dashi stock sachets if you don't want to make your own. Dashi powder, commonly known as dashi no moto, is a salty umami flavoring that may be found in Asian grocers.

Miso

Miso, there are seemingly endless variations of miso paste. You can try darker & lighter misos, and the most significant difference I've noticed is that the lighter, white miso tastes sweeter than the darker miso. Adding a few teaspoons of miso paste to ramen soup tends to bring out the umami flavor. Many cookbooks identify the many types of miso, but you can use what you have. Choose a middle-colored one if you're presented with a vast selection. If you don't have access to an Asian shop, many Waitrose stores offer Clearspring, and their miso soup sachets are used for a miso foundation.

The greatest thing to do here is experiment with various sorts until you discover the one that tastes the finest.

Low-sodium soy sauce

Many of the recipes will include low-sodium soy sauce. The light and dark low-sodium soy sauces in China are not the same as the Japanese low-sodium soy sauce. Light low-sodium soy sauce is salty and used earlier in the cooking process in Chinese cuisine, while black low-sodium soy sauce is used later in the preparation of food for flavoring. When combined, they give a lot of flavor complexity, so you can use a little amount of each.

Rice wine with mirin

Mirin is a sweet rice wine now readily accessible in most supermarkets' foreign food sections. It adds sweetness to a meal and has a dense texture.

Many Japanese meals call for sake, but since it's tough to come by, you can use Chinese Shaoxing rice wine that is more readily accessible. When employing delicate flavors in Chinese & Japanese cuisine, shouxing rice wine provides another depth of complexity, and it's great for seasoning meat and sauces. If you're in need, use dry sherry or even a dab of white wine in the recipes.

Chilli Bean Paste or Chilli Bean Sauce

It is another Chinese & Japanese crossover that is particularly helpful to store in the fridge since it can be used in various dishes. As one can see, it comes in various packaging with different names. You can get the Lee Kum Kee available at Waitrose and is slightly less potent than other thicker pastes. Use a bit less of the Chinese paste if you purchase it. It's made out of a blend of chilies & fermented soybeans, and it's used to give food a spicy, salty flavor. As a huge fan of hot, spicy cuisine, you can use this in a variety of dishes.

Nori

Nori is a kind of Japanese seaweed that is occasionally served to peek out of the edge of a bowl of ramen. It has a crunchy, salty flavor. Individual little packets, freshly cut to size for convenience of use, can be purchased in bulk at Chinese stores for a meager price. If you can't locate it, you may chop down huge nori sheets generally used for sushi wraps. Itsu's seaweed thins, on the other hand, are the same thing. Try Itsu seaweed thins, which are flavored with Japanese horseradish, for a somewhat more robust flavor. You can normally put the nori on the ramen bowl's side so that one end stays crunchy when the other end absorbs the broth's flavor.

Beni shoga (pickled red ginger)

Beni shoga is a vivid red pickled ginger with a rich, sweet taste used as a ramen topping. Beni shoga, which has a punchier, tangier flavor than pinkish sushi ginger, is hard to come across, even at Asian grocers.

It's available at several of London's Chinatown grocers, as well as Japan Centre. If you can get it, it's worth the price since there's no alternative for its crisp, acidic flavor. You usually simply take a forkful, tap the edge of the jar to empty the liquid, and place it in a little pile on 1 side of the ramen dish.

Chilli Oil with Nanami Togarashi

Chilli oil and chili powder may be put on top of the Ramen if you want the food a little hot. La yu is a sesame oil-based Japanese chili oil with a somewhat nutty flavor. For spiciness without the sesame taste, Chinese chili oil may be used.

Nanami togarashi powder, a Japanese blend of sesame seeds & chili powder, also gives a nice kick to dishes. Both may be sprinkled on top of the ramen dish before eating.

Kimchi

It is a salty, acidic Korean fermenting pickled cabbage with a spicy, salty, sour taste. Both the cabbage and its liquid may be utilized to flavor broths, which is particularly useful in more subtle seafood ramen. You can obtain kimchi cooked with a variety of veggies, but the most common is cabbage kimchi. You can use it straight from the jar on the Ramen as a topping in addition to adding it to broths. It's also good with a bowl of simple rice.

Japanese curry sauce

These curry sauce sachets include a bar of curry concentrates that may be broken apart and used to stock bases to make a curried broth. The flavor is comparable to that of Chinese curry, and it produces a wonderful curry broth with a delicate flavor.

2.3 Putting It All Together

Broth: it is the most important. Ramen broth may be prepared up to a week ahead of time, and only one serving of amount can be stored for thawing & consumption at any time. Before eating with the Ramen, bring the broth back to a regular boil.

Seasoning: You may make the fragrant tare combination up to one week ahead of time. This combination can be created and stored on hand at all times since we're using an essential blend of low-sodium soy sauce & mirin. Before eating, add this tare to a saucepan of stock or a single bowl of ramen soup.

Ramen Noodles: Before serving, cook the noodles in boiling water. Gummy noodles might result from boiling the noodles in the broth. Alternatively, boil the noodles in simply water & drain them before adding them to the single-serving soup bowls.

Toppings: Roasted pork, occasionally ground pork, roasting pork loin, or pulled pork, is often put on top of this form of Ramen. You can keep the toppings basic to concentrate the efforts on generating the most extraordinary ramen broth possible. A bowl of ramen needs is a silky-soft cooked egg, maybe pickled bamboo crumbled nori, and a drizzle of sesame oil to make it into a healthy meal.

2.4 Enjoying the Ramen

There is no such thing as a bad way to eat Ramen. Tradition mandates that the Ramen be consumed whereas the soup is still hot, which necessitates getting the lips closer to the bowl and guiding the noodles to the mouth with chopsticks. This is most likely the origin of the noodle slurp. Sucking the noodle into the mouth cools it as it enters the mouth. For drinking the broth and savoring the Ramen's egg topping, a soup spoon may and should be used in combination with chopsticks.

Chapter 3: Tips to Make Home-Cooked Ramen

It's about the noodles & the broth

Toppings are hardly unneeded if the broth & the noodles are proper. Concentrate on infusing the broth with flavor and richness; take your time. If you're not cooking your own noodles, look for the finest ones one can find and purchase them fresh.

The broth's flavor and substance originate from a variety of components.

There should be a lot of bones (and veggies if you wish to make a vegan broth) in the soup pot, which means a lot. Without many components and patience to extract all flavors, you can't obtain a decent taste and a thick broth. Before adding water, fill the stockpot full of components, and after it's done, a few gallons of water should decrease to just a few liters of broth.

Never season the soup with salt or pepper

So broth is blended with a seasoned foundation (tare in Japanese culture). When single-serving bowls of Ramen are made, it is never seasoned. The foundation may be pork braising liquid, tamari, low-sodium soy sauce, dashi, various other ingredients, but the salt is not ever added to the broth itself, ensuring that the finished bowl of Ramen has just one source of flavor.

The ramen noodle boiling water should never be salted.

Ramen noodles are not cooked in salted water for about the same purpose that the broth is not ever salted. This is a break from traditional Italian pasta preparation, but the soup base seasoning has the broth and the noodles when everything is mixed.

Make sure the noodles are thoroughly cooked

Similar to preparing Italian noodles, Ramen should be just cooked through. Overcooked Ramen will be sloppy and pasty, while undercooked Ramen will be rough & floury. Boil the noodles at the last minute when everything else seems prepared, keep an eye on the time, and keep checking the Ramen so that they take out of the water the second they're done.

If you're going to make a broth, use miso.

Combine the miso with boiling water if you want the ramen broth to have the most genuine umami (meaty and tasty). Of course, you may use pig or chicken bones in conjunction with miso for an even fuller flavor. Miso paste may now be found at Asian shops and marketplaces, as well as supermarkets. So, if you're seeking a quick and easy broth recipe, combining a tablespoon of miso paste with boiling water would undoubtedly suffice.

Add an egg to the ramen soup

If there's one element that genuinely distinguishes Japanese Ramen from other quick noodle soups, it's the rich flavor of eggs. Adding an egg to the ramen soup is rather common, and several variations combine boiled, raw, scrambled, & other eggs. That said, one may just break one egg into the boiling stock and simmer it on medium heat until the halves are ready to toss into the liquid, or one can play with the scrambling yellowy deliciousness as it combines with the broth & noodles. Ensure to include the egg in your recipe, no matter which path you choose.

Don't be afraid to include vegetables

Whenever it comes to comfort foods like Ramen, the Japanese aim to eat healthily. This is why the bulk of Asian ramen recipes call for various veggies. Toss in the vegetables a few minutes before the soup is done. The beauty of contemporary cooking is that one can simply purchase a box of frozen vegetable mix that will save you not only money but also time. If you like, you may use fresh veggies. One really can't go wrong with peas, carrots & broccoli, topped with chopped chives and possibly other leafy veggies in season. You may also mix and match various vegetables or stick to a single veggie pick if you want. The joy of Ramen is that one can play around with it until they discover the perfect flavor combination.

Get that protein dose

Japanese Ramen is one of the best comfort meals available today, but it may also keep one full for longer provided you include enough protein. So, in addition to the egg, make sure the Ramen has some meat. Beef or chicken are the most popular choices, although pork & fish are also good. Remember that boneless wrapped pork shoulder is the ideal meat component for flavorful Ramen if you're opting for pork. One can't go wrong with stir-fried tofu if you're seeking a meat-free meal that'll satisfy the appetite just as well.

Add some spice to the mix

When everything is cooked to perfection, season the Ramen to your liking. In principle, adding around a tsp. of low-sodium soy sauce is the most conventional method, but one may adjust the amount to your preference. Furthermore, there is a variety of low-sodium soy sauce tastes to choose from to enhance the flavor and scent of the Ramen. Those who want their Ramen hot & spicy might add chili sauce to the ramen noodles in addition to the saltiness. For spicy cuisine fans, cayenne pepper is also a popular option.

Cook the noodles on the broiler

It's important not to overcook the Ramen while making Japanese-style Ramen. That's why noodles are usually added to the soup at the very end when it has already begun to boil. However, you can take things a step further by broiling the noodles before putting them back into the soup. When the Ramen is ready to eat, pour the broth into a separate pan, remove the noodles, and wrap them in aluminum foil. Preheat the oven to broil, then place the noodles on foil in the oven for 60-120 seconds. Remove the noodles from the oven as soon as possible, return them to the broth, and savor crispier Ramen.

Cook your Ramen in a stir-fry pan

Stir-fried Ramen is a wonderful delicacy that doesn't take up too much time after it's prepared and ready to eat. All one has to do now is take the Ramen from the saucepan, oil the wok, and toss everything in there to stir and cook for a few minutes. If you like the vegetables raw, this is a terrific way to incorporate them into the Ramen while stir-frying so that you can experience the crunchier, more intensified flavor of the veggies as well.

When it comes to food ramen, there is no unique etiquette, but one should understand that it is best to show off their satisfaction in an obvious way. In Japan, however, it is usual to consume this meal rapidly, noisily slurping and consuming all of the noodles & toppings in the bowl. Furthermore, according to Japanese custom, if one completes all of the noodles in a bowl before completing the remainder of the meal, you are entitled to a second helping.

If you're not sure what sort of Ramen you enjoy but have a strong desire to sample a wide variety of cultural Japanese-style ramen dishes, you can start with the book's unforgettable recipes.

3.1 Kitchen Conversions

SPOONS & CUPS

TSP	TBSP	FL OZ	CUP
3	1	1/2	1/16
6	2	1	1/8
12	4	2	1/4
18	6	3	3/8
24	8	4	1/2
36	12	6	3/4
48	16	8	1

MILLILITERS

TSP	ML
1/2	2.5
1	5

TBSP	ML
1	15

OZ	ML
2	60
4	115
6	150
8	230
10	285
12	340

CUP	ML
1/4	60
1/2	120
2/3	160
3/4	180
1	240

GRAMS

OZ	G	LB
2	58	-
4	114	-
6	170	-
8	226	1/2
12	340	-
16	454	1

Chapter 4: Classic Ramen Recipes

Chicken Ramen

Prep Time	Cooking Time	Servings
1 h 10 min	40 min	4

Ingredients

Caramelized Soy Chicken

MARINADE

¼ tsp of cayenne pepper
2 tbsp of mirin
1 tbsp of dark low-sodium soy sauce
4 chicken thigh with skin & boneless
1 tbsp of light low-sodium soy sauce
2 garlic cloves, minced

GLAZE

2 tbsp of dark low-sodium soy sauce
2 tsp of brown sugar

CLASSIC RAMEN

4 to 5 cups of chicken stock
4 spring onions' stalks, chopped
4 to 5 garlic cloves
2" piece of ginger, thinly sliced
1½ tbsp of red pepper flakes
¼ cup of each light low-sodium soy sauce
& mirin
6 to 8 oz. of shiitake mushrooms, sliced
without stems
12 to 13 oz. of dried 4 portions of ramen
noodles
4 soft boiled eggs

STEAMED GREENS

Garlic, as needed
2 bunches of spinach
Low-sodium soy sauce, as needed
Sesame oil, as needed
Ramen toppings
Chili garlic oil, as needed
Sliced radishes, as needed
4 spring onions' stalks, sliced
Ramen eggs, as needed

Instructions

1. In a bowl, add all the marinade ingredients. Mix well & add chicken.
2. Let it rest for 1 hour.
3. Let the oven preheat to 425 F.
4. Add the chicken to a parchment-lined baking sheet, skinless side down, place in the upper third of the oven.
5. Roast for 15 minutes. Meanwhile, mix the glaze's ingredients.
6. Flip the chicken brush with glaze & roast for 10 to 15 minutes more. Take it out of the oven & cool. Slice & set it aside.
7. For ramen, in one pan, add the garlic, chili, low-sodium soy sauce, stock, green onion, mirin & ginger. Cook for 20-25 minutes on medium flame. Taste & adjust seasoning.
8. In another pot, add water & boil. Cook noodles as per the package instructions. Drain & add to the serving bowls.
9. From the simmering pot, remove the garlic & ginger. Stain & add the mushrooms; cook for 5 minutes.
10. Pour over the noodles, serve with a soft boiled egg.

NUTRITION PER SERVINGS			
CALORIES	PROTEIN	CARBS	FAT
120 kcal	4 g	19 g	21 g

Homemade Shoyu Ramen

Prep Time	Cooking Time	Servings
30 min	**60 min**	**4**

Ingredients

FOR CHICKEN DASHI (STOCK)

16 dried shiitake mushrooms
20g of dried bonito flakes
30g of kombu (kelp)
8 cups of chicken broth

FOR TARE & CHASHU

1¼ cup of mirin
Half cup of sake
1 two-inch piece of ginger, sliced
1¼ cup of light low-sodium soy sauce
1½ cups of water
3 peeled cloves of garlic, smashed
¼ cup of granulated sugar
2 tbsp of brown sugar
1 lb. of pork belly, with skin, cut into 2"
wide pieces
3 green onions, cut in half

FOR NITAMAGO

2½ cups of chashu-tare liquid
4 eggs
For Garlic La-Yu
Half cup of canola oil
2 tsp of sesame seeds
1½ tbsp of red pepper flakes
8 sliced cloves of garlic

FOR EACH SERVING

2 shiitake mushrooms, cut into slices
2 tsp of la-yu
1½ cup of chicken dashi
1 nitamago, cut in half
1 green onion, sliced thin
2 slices of chashu
3 tbsp of tare, or more
4 oz. fresh ramen noodles

Instructions

1. To make dashi, add chicken broth to a pan. Simmer on medium flame, turn the heat off & cool for 2 minutes.
2. Add kombu & mushrooms, steep for 5 minutes.
3. Add flakes & let it steep for 5 minutes. Strain & let it rest. Use within one week.
4. For chashu & tare, add all ingredients to a pan. Do not add pork yet; simmer on low flame.
5. In another pot, add pork with 6 cups of water, simmer on low flame. Drain & rinse the pork.
6. Add the pork to the tare pot, simmer for 1 hour & 20 minutes on low until tender.
7. Cool for 20 minutes, strain. Keep in the fridge separately, pork & liquid.
8. Before serving, slice & torch the pork slices.
9. In a pan, add water to boil. Add the eggs & simmer for 6 minutes. Drain & add to the ice water for 10 minutes, then peel.
10. Add the eggs to a bowl, cover with pork liquid. Weigh them down with kombu. Keep in the fridge for 4-12 hours.
11. In a pan, add oil & garlic, cook on the lowest flame. Cook for 15 minutes; make sure not to brown the garlic.
12. Turn the heat off & add the chili. Let it rest for 2 minutes add sesame. Use within 2 weeks.
13. Cook the ramen as per the package instructions. Drain.
14. In a pan, add dashi & mushrooms, cook for 60 seconds, until simmering. Turn the heat off.
15. In a bowl, add all the ingredients after adding noodles. Serve & enjoy.

NUTRITION PER SERVINGS			
CALORIES	**PROTEIN**	**CARBS**	**FAT**
213 kcal	*5 g*	*21 g*	*17 g*

Quick Homemade Ramen

Prep Time	Cooking Time	Servings
10 min	15 min	6

Ingredients

3 tsp of grated ginger
4 tsp of grated garlic
2 portions of instant ramen
2 cups of chopped kale
4 cups of any broth
Crunchy panko crumbs, for serving
4 cups of water
1 oz. of dried shiitake mushrooms
1 tbsp of sesame oil
1 cup of shredded carrots
3 soft boiled eggs, cut in half
Half cup of chopped scallions or chives
Sriracha, to taste

Instructions

1. Sauté the ginger, garlic in hot sesame oil for 2 minutes.
2. Add water & broth, simmer & add mushrooms. Cook for 10 minutes.
3. Add the instant noodles, cook for 5 minutes or until they soften.
4. Add the green onion & mix well. Turn the heat off, add carrots & kale.
5. Serve with egg & panko crumbs on top.
6. Add low-sodium soy sauce, chili oil & sesame oil to taste.
7. In a pot, add water & boil.
8. Add eggs & cook for 6 minutes, turn the heat off & immediately transfer to ice-cold water.
9. Let it rest for few minutes, peel & cut in half. Serve with ramen.

NUTRITION PER SERVINGS			
CALORIES	**PROTEIN**	**CARBS**	**FAT**
309 kcal	*15 g*	*12 g*	*8 g*

Classic Shoyu Ramen

Prep Time	Cooking Time	Servings
15 min	**35 min**	**2**

Ingredients

SOUP BASE

1 piece of kombu
2 cups of chicken stock
Half cup of bonito flakes

SHOYU TARE

1 clove garlic, grated
3 tbsp of shoyu
1 tbsp of sesame oil
2 tsp of grated ginger
1 tsp of mirin

RAMEN TOPPINGS & ASSEMBLY

2 pieces of fermented bamboo shoots
4 slices of chashu
1 soft boiled egg, cut in half
6 slices of fish cakes
10 oz. of fresh ramen noodles
Chili oil, to serve
1 tbsp of sesame seeds, roughly coarse
2 pieces of nori
2 scallions, sliced thin

Instructions

1. In a pan, add the water (2 cups) & kombu, let it simmer.
2. Turn the heat off & take the kombu out. Turn the heat on & add the bonito flakes.
3. Let it come to a simmer, turn the heat off. Let it rest for 10 minutes, covered. Strain & set it aside.
4. In a pan, add the chicken stock with the prepared stock. Place on low flame & keep warm.
5. In a pan, heat the oil on medium-high heat. Add the ginger, garlic cook for 30 seconds.
6. Add the mirin with low-sodium soy sauce, turn the heat off. It is shoyu tare.
7. Add the tare to the chicken-dashi stock only 1 tbsp at a time and adjust to your taste.
8. Cook ramen as per package instructions & drain.
9. Add to the bowl add the rest of the ingredients on top.
10. Serve with desired toppings.
11. In a pot, add water & boil.
12. Add egg & cook for 6 minutes, turn the heat off & immediately transfer to ice-cold water.
13. Let it rest for few minutes, peel & cut in half. Serve with ramen.

NUTRITION PER SERVINGS			
CALORIES	**PROTEIN**	**CARBS**	**FAT**
230 kcal	*16 g*	*17 g*	*8 g*

Easy Pork Ramen

Prep Time	Cooking Time	Servings
15 min	**35 min**	**2**

Ingredients

PORK

1.5 lb. of Roasted Pork Tenderloin (with garlic & black peppercorn)

RAMEN NOODLES

4 cups of beef broth low-salt
1 to 2 slices of ginger
1½ tsp of black peppercorns, coarse ground
2 to 3 garlic cloves
2 soft boiled eggs
2 portions of dried ramen noodles
2 spring onions, slice into larger pieces
2 to 4 stalks of chinese greens
½ tbsp of chili flakes, or to taste
1 to 2 tbsp of low-sodium soy sauce
4 oz. of shiitakes mushrooms, thinly sliced

Instructions

1. In a pan, add all the ingredients except for Asian greens, green onion, noodles & mushrooms.
2. Let it come to a boil, cover & simmer on a medium flame for 15 to 20 minutes.
3. Take the pork out & thinly slice.
4. Add the greens & cook for 1 to 2 minutes; take them out
5. Add the noodles with mushrooms, cook for 3 to 5 minutes.
6. For serving, add the noodles with broth in 2 bowls.
7. Add the rest of the ingredients. Serve.
8. In a pot, add water & boil.
9. Add eggs & cook for 6 minutes, turn the heat off & immediately transfer to ice-cold water.
10. Let it rest for few minutes, peel & cut in half. Serve with ramen.

NUTRITION PER SERVINGS			
CALORIES	**PROTEIN**	**CARBS**	**FAT**
256 kcal	*21 g*	*13 g*	*6 g*

Classic Tonkotsu Ramen

Prep Time	Cooking Time	Servings
15 min	**35 min**	**2**

Ingredients

SOUP BASE

1" piece of ginger, unpeeled
2 green onions
1 pound of split pig's trotters
Half onion, cut into fours, unpeeled

TO ASSEMBLE

Low-sodium soy sauce, to taste
7 oz. of fresh ramen noodles
¼ cup of green onions, thinly sliced
2 pieces of nori
4 slices of chashu pork
Sea salt, to taste
¼ cup of enoki mushrooms
Chili oil, to taste
2 pieces of fermented bamboo shoots
1 tbsp low-sodium soy sauce
1 tbsp of sesame seeds, roughly ground
2 soft boiled eggs, cut in half

Instructions

1. In a pot, add the trotters and water to cover them.
2. Let it come to a boil, turn the heat off. Drain. Clean under cold water, add to a pot.
3. In a pan, on a medium flame, add the yellow onion, ginger & green onion. Sauté until slightly charred.
4. Add to the trotters' pot add water to cover them.
5. Let it come to a boil, simmer on low flame for 20 minutes.
6. Add more water & simmer for 6 hours. Boil & cook to desired thickness.
7. Strain & keep in the fridge overnight.
8. Before serving, add the broth to a pan with fat & simmer.
9. Add salt & low-sodium soy sauce.
10. Cook noodles as per package instructions. Drain & add to the serving bowls.
11. Add the broth with the rest of the ingredients on top.
12. In a pot, add water & boil.
13. Add eggs & cook for 6 minutes, turn the heat off & immediately transfer to ice-cold water.
14. Let it rest for few minutes, peel & cut in half. Serve with ramen.
15. Serve & enjoy.

NUTRITION PER SERVINGS			
CALORIES	**PROTEIN**	**CARBS**	**FAT**
312 kcal	*25 g*	*14 g*	*14 g*

Spicy Pork Ramen Noodle Soup

Prep Time	Cooking Time	Servings
20 min	**4 h 40 min**	**4**

Ingredients

2.2 lbs of rolled pork shoulder
2 peeled carrots, 1 whole & 1 cut into matchsticks
¼ tsp of pepper
8½ cups of chicken stock
1 onion, unpeeled & halved
¼ tsp of salt
1 celery stick, halved
3 cloves garlic, unpeeled & halved
1" piece of ginger, unpeeled & chopped
2 tbsp of olive oil
3 tbsp of low-sodium soy sauce
2 tbsp of Gochujang Paste, or to taste
1 tsp of black sesame seeds
4 eggs
7 oz. of dried ramen noodles
2 tbsp of mirin
1 red chili, sliced with or without seeds
1 leek, sliced
3 packed cups of baby spinach leaves
1 tsp of red chili flakes
1 tsp of white sesame seeds
Scallions, sliced

Instructions

1. Let the oven preheat to 300 F. In a pan, heat 1 tbsp of oil.
2. With salt & pepper, season the pork. Sear the pork on all sides.
3. Add the stock on top of the pork.
4. Add ginger, onion, celery, garlic & whole carrot.
5. Add the red chili, mirin, and gochujang & low-sodium soy sauce. Let it come to a boil, keep in the oven for 4 hours after covering with a lid.
6. Add more water if needed; keep checking. In the end, it needs to have 1 liter of liquid.
7. Take the pot out & place the pork on a cutting board. Take the fat layer off.
8. Shred the meat finely & strain the liquid. Discard the solids.
9. Boil the eggs for six minutes & transfer to the ice-cold water.
10. Cook the noodles as per package instructions.
11. Add some oil to a pan. Sauté leek with a pinch of pepper & salt for 5 minutes.
12. Add the spinach to the pan after pushing the leeks on one side. Let it cook for 1 minute.
13. Add the cooked noodles to the serving bowls. Add the pork, spinach mixture, carrots & broth.
14. Cut the eggs in half & place them on top. Serve with the rest of the ingredients on top.

NUTRITION PER SERVINGS			
CALORIES	**PROTEIN**	**CARBS**	**FAT**
670 kcal	45 g	53 g	30 g

Braised Pork Ramen

Prep Time	Cooking Time	Servings
20 min	**4 h 40 min**	**6**

Ingredients

1 tbsp + 2 tsp of vegetable oil
2 pounds of pork butt (boneless), halved
Half cup of low-sodium soy sauce
10 cloves garlic (3 cloves minced & 7 smashed)
⅓ cup of mirin
4 dried shiitake mushrooms
1 onion, cut in half
6 scallions, cut in half
4" of unpeeled ginger, sliced & smashed
2½ pounds of chicken wings, split
6 portions of dried ramen noodles
6 oz. of thick-cut bacon
Kosher salt, to taste
3 eggs, soft-boiled

Instructions

1. Let the broiler preheat.
2. Toss the onion with 2 tsp of oil & broil for 12 minutes.
3. Change the oven's temperature to 275 F.
4. In a Dutch oven, add 1 tbsp of oil, add pork & cook for 8 minutes.
5. Add water (¾ cup), 3 minced garlic cloves, mirin, low-sodium soy sauce, ¼th of the ginger & 2 scallions.
6. Let it come to a boil, placing in the oven after placing a lid on top.
7. Cook for 2 to 3 hours, keep flipping the pork after each hour. Strain the liquid & shred the pork.
8. In a pot, add 10 cups of water with bacon & wings.
9. Boil for 3 minutes on high flame, take the foam off & simmer on low for 1 hour.
10. Add the dried shiitakes, smashed garlic, broiled onion, 4 green onion & the rest of the ginger.
11. Simmer for 60 minutes, stirring as needed.
12. Strain & add to a different pot; it needs to be 8 cups. Add the strained pork stock.
13. Add salt to taste, place on a low flame.
14. Cook the noodles as per package instructions. Slice the pork thickly.
15. Add some of the minced garlic, cooked noodles in each serving bowl.
16. Pour the broth with pork.
17. In a pot, add water & boil.
18. Add eggs & cook for 6 minutes, turn the heat off & immediately transfer to ice-cold water.
19. Let it rest for few minutes, peel & cut in half. Serve with ramen.
20. Serve & enjoy.

NUTRITION PER SERVINGS			
CALORIES	**PROTEIN**	**CARBS**	**FAT**
312 kcal	*25 g*	*21 g*	*16 g*

Slow Cooker Pork Ramen

Prep Time	Cooking Time	Servings
20 min	**8-10 h 40 min**	**8**

Ingredients

MARINADE

2 tsp of fish sauce, 2 tsp of kosher salt
2 pounds of pork shoulder, boneless
2 tsp of sesame oil
2 tsp of packed brown sugar
2 tsp of rice vinegar

FOR THE SLOW COOKER

2 peeled carrots, halved
2 stalks celery, halved
6 smashed cloves garlic
2" of ginger, peeled
1 onion, chopped
2 tbsp of packed brown sugar
¼ cup of rice vinegar
1 jalapeno, cut in half without seeds
3 tbsp of chicken bouillon
½ cup + 2 tbsp of low-sodium soy sauce
1 tbsp of fish sauce
16 oz. of ramen noodles
1 tsp of sriracha, 11 cups of water

SAUTEÉD TOPPINGS

2 carrots, sliced into matchsticks
pinch of salt
1 leek, chopped, 2 tsp of olive oil
5 oz. of baby spinach, roughly chopped

FOR CRISPY PORK

2 tbsp of low-sodium soy sauce
2 tbsp of packed brown sugar
2 tbsp of sesame oil, 2 tbsp of rice vinegar

GARNISHES

Sesame seeds & red pepper flakes, as needed
1 jalapeno, sliced
4 green onions, thinly sliced
1 cup of corn
4 eggs, soft-boiled

Instructions

1. Cut the pork shoulder into 2-3 pieces. Add to a zip lock bag, season with 2 tsp of kosher salt. Coat well.
2. Add the sesame oil, brown sugar, rice vinegar & fish sauce (2 tsp of each) to the pork. Shake well. Let it rest for half an hour.
3. In a slow cooker, add all the ingredients with the pork.
4. Add 2 tbsp + half cup of each low-sodium soy sauce, 2 tbsp of brown sugar, 1 tbsp of fish sauce, 1 tsp of sriracha, ¼ cup of rice vinegar with 3 tbsp. of chicken base & water (11 cups).
5. Mix & cook for 8 to 10 hours on low. Take the pork out & shred.
6. Take the vegetables out & discard them. Cook the broth on high.
7. 20 minutes before serving, add the ramen to the slow cooker. Cook for 15 to 20 minutes.
8. Sauté the vegetables & set them aside.
9. Serve the noodles with broth, shredded pork, sautéed vegetables & desired toppings.
10. In a pot, add water & boil.
11. Add eggs & cook for 6 minutes, turn the heat off & immediately transfer to ice-cold water.
12. Let it rest for few minutes, peel & cut in half. Serve with ramen.
13. Serve & enjoy.

NUTRITION PER SERVINGS			
CALORIES	**PROTEIN**	**CARBS**	**FAT**
309 kcal	23 g	27 g	14 g

Shio Ramen

Prep Time	Cooking Time	Servings
20 min	20 min	2

Ingredients

SHIO TARE

Pinch of bonito flakes
1 tsp of mirin
1 tbsp of sea salt
Half of one kombu

TO ASSEMBLE

⅔ cup of dashi stock
8 oz. of ramen noodles
1⅓ cup of chicken broth
2 pieces of fermented bamboo shoots
2 tsp of sesame oil
4 slices of chashu
2 scallions, sliced
2 strips of nori
1 soft boiled egg, halved

Instructions

1. In a pan, add water (1 cup) & salt. Let it boil on medium flame until dissolved.
2. Add the kombu & mirin, turn the heat off. Place a lid on top & rest for 5 minutes.
3. Take the kombu out & heat it well. Add the bonito flakes, let it steep for 3 minutes.
4. Strain the liquid.
5. In a pan, add stock & chicken broth, let it simmer on low.
6. Cook the noodles as per package instructions.
7. Add the tare to the chicken stock's mixture.
8. In each serving bowl, add 1 tsp of sesame oil. Add the cooked noodles.
9. Add the soup on top with desired toppings. Serve.
10. In a pot, add water & boil.
11. Add eggs & cook for 6 minutes, turn the heat off & immediately transfer to ice-cold water.
12. Let it rest for few minutes, peel & cut in half. Serve with ramen.
13. Serve & enjoy.

NUTRITION PER SERVINGS			
CALORIES	**PROTEIN**	**CARBS**	**FAT**
312 kcal	*19.8 g*	*15 g*	*11 g*

Rich and Creamy Tonkotsu Ramen

Prep Time	Cooking Time	Servings
20 min	**10 h 20 min**	**6-8**

Ingredients

1 onion, unpeeled & chopped
3 pounds of pig trotters, cut into 1" of disks
2 tbsp of vegetable oil
2 dozens of scallions, white parts only
1 pound of slab pork fat back
12 garlic cloves
1 three-inch piece of ginger, chopped
2 pounds of chicken carcasses & backs, without skin & fat
2 whole leeks, chopped
6 oz. of whole mushrooms
3-4 soft boiled eggs, cut in half

Instructions

1. In a pot, add chicken bones & pork with water.
2. Let it come to a boil. Turn the heat off & drain. Wash under water & clean well.
3. In a pan, heat the oil and sauté ginger, onion & garlic. Cook for 15 minutes.
4. Add the cleaned trotters to a pot with pork fatback, garlic mixture & other vegetables.
5. Add water to cover the ingredients & boil over high flame, remove the scum off the top.
6. Turn the heat low & simmer with a lid on top; cook for 4 hours.
7. Take the pork fat out & keep in the fridge. Cook the broth for 6-8 hours more. Add more water if needed to keep the bones submerged.
8. Cook on high heat at the end until it is reduced by 3 quarts. Strain & do not use the solids.
9. Chop the pork fatback & add to the strained broth.
10. Cook the noodles as per package instructions. Serve the ramen with broth & other desired toppings.
11. In a pot, add water & boil.
12. Add eggs & cook for 6 minutes, turn the heat off & immediately transfer to ice-cold water.
13. Let it rest for few minutes, peel & cut in half. Serve with ramen.
14. Serve & enjoy.

NUTRITION PER SERVINGS			
CALORIES	**PROTEIN**	**CARBS**	**FAT**
312 kcal	*23 g*	*21 g*	*22 g*

Shoyu Ramen with Corn & Choy Sum

Prep Time	Cooking Time	Servings
20 min	2h 20 min	6-8

Ingredients

1" piece of ginger, sliced
2 scallions, sliced thin & color separated
2 tsp of sesame oil
2 liters of chicken stock
2 tbsp of mirin
2 garlic cloves, sliced
⅓ cup of low-sodium soy sauce
6 whole dried shiitake mushrooms, soaked in water, then drained
1 bunch of choy sum, trimmed
2 tbsp of cooking sake
2 tsp of dried chili flakes
2 chicken breast fillets
270g dried somen noodles
1 cup of sweet corn kernels
3-4 soft-boiled eggs
Half sheet of nori
1 tbsp of sesame seeds
Sesame seed sprinkle

Instructions

1. Sauté the garlic, white part of the scallion & ginger. Cook for 2 minutes.
2. Add low-sodium soy sauce, mirin, mushrooms, stock & sake. Let it come to a boil, turn the heat low.
3. Add chicken & simmer for 12 to 13 minutes. Take the chicken out & slice thin.
4. Strain the broth & only reserve the mushrooms.
5. Cook noodles as per package instructions.
6. Add the broth to a pan with choy sum & corn. Cook for 2 minutes.
7. Toast nori for half a minute on medium flame in a pan. Take it out on a plate, do the same to the sesame seeds.
8. Add the seeds & nori to the bowl. Add the mushrooms, chicken & noodles.
9. Pour the hot stock on top.
10. Serve with desired toppings.
11. In a pot, add water & boil.
12. Add eggs & cook for 6 minutes, turn the heat off & immediately transfer to ice-cold water.
13. Let it rest for few minutes, peel & cut in half. Serve with ramen.
14. Serve & enjoy.

NUTRITION PER SERVINGS			
CALORIES	**PROTEIN**	**CARBS**	**FAT**
268 kcal	23 g	13.8 g	11 g

Beef Ramen Noodle Soup

Prep Time	Cooking Time	Servings
20 min	**2h 20 min**	**6-8**

Ingredients

4 oz. of choy sum
3 tbsp of beef demi-glace
4 cloves garlic
3 tbsp of white miso paste
3 scallions
9 oz. of flank steak
2 oz. of enoki mushrooms
12 oz. of fresh ramen noodles
1" piece of ginger
2 tbsp of low-sodium soy sauce
⅛ cup of hoisin sauce
3-4 soft boiled eggs, cut in half

Instructions

1. Cut the choy sum into small pieces, cut the leaves into bigger pieces.
2. Peel & mince the ginger & garlic. Slice the green onions, separate them via colors.
3. Cut the enoki mushrooms' root.
4. Season the steak with black pepper & salt. In a pot, add 2 tsp of oil.
5. Sear the steak for 3-4 minutes on each side. Take it out on a plate, let it rest for 5 minutes.
6. Add olive oil (2 tsp) in the pan, sauté ginger, white scallion & garlic for 1-2 minutes.
7. Add choy sum and season with black pepper & salt. Cook for 1-3 minutes.
8. Add the water (4 cups), enoki mushrooms, low-sodium soy sauce, beef demi-glace & miso paste, turn the heat to high.
9. Let it come to a boil, turn the heat to low, simmer for 4-5 minutes.
10. Slice the beef & coat with hoisin sauce.
11. Cook the ramen until tender. Drain & add to the serving bowl.
12. Add the soup & steak on top with scallions. Serve.
13. In a pot, add water & boil.
14. Add eggs & cook for 6 minutes, turn the heat off & immediately transfer to ice-cold water.
15. Let it rest for few minutes, peel & cut in half. Serve with ramen.
16. Serve & enjoy.

NUTRITION PER SERVINGS			
CALORIES	**PROTEIN**	**CARBS**	**FAT**
289 kcal	*22 g*	*16 g*	*15 g*

Thai Chicken & Ramen

Prep Time	Cooking Time	Servings
20 min	40 min	6-8

Ingredients

4 cups of chicken stock
1 tbsp of lime juice
1 can of (400ml) coconut milk
2 chicken breast fillets
¼ cup of curry paste, yellow or red
180g of ramen noodles
100g of snow peas, sliced thin
4 scallions, sliced into long matchsticks
125g of baby corn, halved lengthways
1 tbsp of brown sugar
2 tsp of fish sauce
1 peeled carrot, sliced into long matchsticks
3-4 soft boiled eggs, cut in half

Instructions

1. In a pan, add the curry paste on a high flame.
2. Cook for half a minute, add stock & coconut milk. Let it come to a simmer.
3. Turn the heat to low. Add chicken & cook for 15 minutes.
4. Take the chicken out & cool for 10 minutes, shred it.
5. Add the corn & noodles to the pot. Simmer for 5 minutes, turn the heat off.
6. Add fish sauce, sugar & lime juice. Season to taste.
7. Serve with scallion, snow peas & carrot on top.
8. In a pot, add water & boil.
9. Add eggs & cook for 6 minutes, turn the heat off & immediately transfer to ice-cold water.
10. Let it rest for few minutes, peel & cut in half. Serve with ramen.
11. Serve & enjoy.

NUTRITION PER SERVINGS			
CALORIES	PROTEIN	CARBS	FAT
309 kcal	26 g	19.1 g	12 g

Spicy Beef Chashu Ramen Noodles

Prep Time	Cooking Time	Servings
20 min	**1h 30 min**	**6-8**

Ingredients

4 portion of fresh ramen noodles
¼ cup of low-sodium soy sauce
1 tbsp of beef stock powder
5 red chili peppers
5 cloves garlic
400g of beef shank
4 shallots
1" piece of ginger, sliced thin
1 stalk of scallion, chopped
1 tbsp of sugar
Hot chili oil, as needed
1 tbsp of cooking oil
8 cups of water
Salt & black pepper, to taste

TOPPINGS

Red chili pepper, chopped
1 pack of enoki mushroom blanched
3-4 soft boiled eggs
Green onion, chopped

Instructions

1. Add the beef shank to a cooker with oil, cook on all sides until browned.
2. Add sugar, ginger, shallot, chili pepper, beef stock powder, low-sodium soy sauce, black pepper, garlic, water (6 cups) & scallions. Let it come to a boil.
3. Cook with pressure for 45 to 60 minutes, as per steak's thickness. Take the meat out & slice thinly.
4. Cook noodles as per package instructions.
5. Boil the soup, add sugar & salt. Stir well.
6. In each serving bowl, add the broth. Add noodles, beef chashu, scallion, enoki mushroom, hot oil & chili.
7. In a pot, add water & boil.
8. Add eggs & cook for 6 minutes, turn the heat off & immediately transfer to ice-cold water.
9. Let it rest for few minutes, peel & cut in half. Serve with ramen.
10. Serve & enjoy.

NUTRITION PER SERVINGS			
CALORIES	**PROTEIN**	**CARBS**	**FAT**
312 kcal	*25 g*	*16 g*	*8 g*

Thinly Sliced Beef Ramen Soup

Prep Time	Cooking Time	Servings
20 min	**1h 30 min**	**3-4**

Ingredients

Half lb. of egg noodles, cooked & cooled
1½ oz. of grated ginger
Salt & black pepper, to taste
2 tbsp of low-sodium soy sauce
2 crushed garlic cloves
14 oz. of beef flank
2 oz. of spring onions, thinly sliced & color-separated
5 cups of beef broth
2 tbsp of vegetable oil
1 tsp of brown sugar
2 soft boiled eggs, cut in half
3½ oz. of snow peas

Instructions

1. Let the oven preheat to 360 F.
2. Season the beef with salt & pepper. Sear the steak in 1 tbsp of hot oil for 3 minutes on all sides.
3. Place on an oil sprayed baking sheet, and roast for 8 minutes.
4. Add some oil to a pot, sauté white scallion, ginger & garlic until translucent.
5. Add broth, low-sodium soy sauce & sugar. Boil for 8 minutes.
6. Thinly slice the roasted beef. Add the noodles & snow peas to the broth, simmer for 5 minutes.
7. Add salt & pepper to taste.
8. Add noodles to the bowl, top with sliced beef & other ingredients & serve.
9. In a pot, add water & boil.
10. Add eggs & cook for 6 minutes, turn the heat off & immediately transfer to ice-cold water.
11. Let it rest for few minutes, peel & cut in half. Serve with ramen.
12. Serve & enjoy.

NUTRITION PER SERVINGS			
CALORIES	**PROTEIN**	**CARBS**	**FAT**
626 kcal	*46 g*	*63 g*	*20 g*

Japanese Ramen Balls

Prep Time	Cooking Time	Servings
20 min	**30 min**	**4-6**

Ingredients

4 tbsp of low-sodium soy sauce
1 tbsp of sesame oil
500g of lean beef mince
1 tbsp of corn flour
2 tbsp of mirin
1½ tsp of caster sugar
1 clove garlic, minced
75g of shiitake mushrooms, sliced
900 ml of beef stock
Salt & black pepper, to taste
180g of ramen noodles
2 tsp of chilli oil
300g of fresh spinach
2-3 soft boiled eggs, cut in half

Instructions

1. In a bowl, add garlic, cornflour, beef, caster sugar (1 tsp), low-sodium soy sauce (half) & sesame oil. Mix well.
2. Make the mixture into 32 balls.
3. In a pan, add the rest of the low-sodium soy sauce, chili oil, stock, sugar & mirin. Let it come to a boil.
4. Add the meatballs & cook for 5 minutes.
5. Add noodles & mushrooms, simmer for 4 minutes.
6. Add spinach, cook for 30 seconds.
7. In a pot, add water & boil.
8. Add eggs & cook for 6 minutes, turn the heat off & immediately transfer to ice-cold water.
9. Let it rest for few minutes, peel & cut in half. Serve with ramen.
10. Serve & enjoy.

NUTRITION PER SERVINGS			
CALORIES	**PROTEIN**	**CARBS**	**FAT**
267 kcal	*26 g*	*25 g*	*21 g*

Rump Steak Chili Miso Ramen

Prep Time	Cooking Time	Servings
20 min	**1h 30 min**	**2**

Ingredients

2 spring onions
1 tsp of red chilli flakes
2 tbsp of white miso paste
2 egg noodle nests
15g of fresh root ginger
1 egg, soft-boiled
5g of black sesame seeds
200g of pak choi
15 ml of rice vinegar
2 garlic cloves
1 carrot
8 ml of low-sodium soy sauce
2 x 150g rump pavé steak
Instructions

Instructions

1. Chop the garlic, spring onion & ginger. Peel & grate the carrots.
2. Cut the pak choi's roots, separate leaves & chop, do not use the roots.
3. Sauté the ginger, chili flakes, garlic & miso paste in hot oil. Cook for half a minute.
4. Add 1.4 liters of water & mix well; add sugar (1-2 tsp), low-sodium soy sauce & vinegar. Let it simmer.
5. Season the steak with salt & sear in hot oil for 2-6 minutes on each side.
6. Take it out on a plate, add the egg noodles to the broth, let it boil on high flame.
7. Cook for 4 to 5 minutes, add pak choi & cook for 1 to 2 minutes. Turn the heat off.
8. Slice the beef thinly.
9. Serve the noodles with beef & the other ingredients on top.
10. In a pot, add water & boil.
11. Add egg & cook for 6 minutes, turn the heat off & immediately transfer to ice-cold water.
12. Let it rest for few minutes, peel & cut in half. Serve with ramen.
13. Serve & enjoy.

NUTRITION PER SERVINGS			
CALORIES	**PROTEIN**	**CARBS**	**FAT**
321 kcal	*23 g*	*25 g*	*13 g*

Beef Udon

Prep Time	Cooking Time	Servings
20 min	**1h 30 min**	**2**

Ingredients

6 to 8 oz. of sliced thin beef
1 tbsp of oil
2 portions of udon noodles
1-2 green onion, white part only
1 soft boiled egg, cut in half

FOR BEEF

2 tsp of sugar
1 tbsp of low-sodium soy sauce

FOR SOUP

1½ tbsp of low-sodium soy sauce
⅛ tsp of kosher salt
1 tbsp of mirin
2½ cups of dashi
1 tsp of sugar

Instructions

1. Cook noodles as per package instructions.
2. Pour dashi in a pan, let it come to a boil. Add salt, low-sodium soy sauce, mirin & sugar. Mix well & turn the heat off.
3. In a pan, add oil on medium flame. Sauté the onion until tender, add meat & cook until done.
4. Add low-sodium soy sauce & sugar. Cook until done, turn the heat off.
5. Add the noodles to serving bowls and pour the soup with beef.
6. Serve with desired toppings on top.
7. In a pot, add water & boil.
8. Add egg & cook for 6 minutes, turn the heat off & immediately transfer to ice-cold water.
9. Let it rest for few minutes, peel & cut in half. Serve with ramen.
10. Serve & enjoy.

NUTRITION PER SERVINGS			
CALORIES	**PROTEIN**	**CARBS**	**FAT**
579 kcal	*32 g*	*59 g*	*8 g*

Chicken & Mushroom Ramen

Prep Time	Cooking Time	Servings
20 min	**30 min**	**4**

Ingredients

1 tsp of olive oil
1½ tsp of chinese five-spice
1 tbsp of dark low-sodium soy sauce
1" piece of ginger, chopped
2 chicken breasts
1 carrot, sliced into thin strips
1.5 liters of hot chicken stock
300g of mixed wild mushrooms, whole or halved
6 spring onions, sliced
1 tbsp of worcestershire sauce
2 garlic cloves, chopped
375g of fresh egg noodles
1 tbsp of miso paste
150g of shredded greens
2 eggs, soft-boiled

Instructions

1. Coat the chicken in oil & season with half tsp of chinese five-spice.
2. Cook chicken in the pan for 5 to 6 minutes on one side. Take it out of the pan & slice thickly.
3. In a pestle & mortar, add the ginger, grind it well.
4. In a pan, add the low-sodium soy sauces, ginger paste, five-spices, Worcestershire, mushrooms, garlic, miso & the stock. Let it come to a boil, simmer for 7 minutes.
5. Cook noodles as per package instructions.
6. In each serving bowl, add the noodles, greens, carrots. Add the broth on top with chicken.
7. Serve with scallions on top.
8. In a pot, add water & boil.
9. Add eggs & cook for 6 minutes, turn the heat off & immediately transfer to ice-cold water.
10. Let it rest for few minutes, peel & cut in half. Serve with ramen.
11. Serve & enjoy.

NUTRITION PER SERVINGS			
CALORIES	**PROTEIN**	**CARBS**	**FAT**
282 kcal	*23.5 g*	*33.5 g*	*6 g*

Ramen with Pan-Seared Wagyu

Prep Time	Cooking Time	Servings
20 min	1h 30 min	4

Ingredients

1 tsp of togarashi seasoning
4 eggs, soft-boiled
1 piece of nori, broken into small pieces
1 bunch of green onion, cut into ¼"
pieces
1 wagyu ribeye
1 can of bamboo shoots, without liquid
8 to 10 shiitake mushrooms, sliced
thinly
3 portions of fresh ramen noodles
1 quart of each beef stock & chicken
stock
2 cups of water
¼ cup of low-sodium soy sauce
4 dry of shiitake mushrooms
1 tbsp of sriracha
1" of ginger, sliced
1 celery stalk, diced large
4 garlic cloves, smashed & peeled
1 yellow onion, diced large
1 carrot, diced large

Instructions

1. Make sure to keep the frozen steak in the fridge for 24 hours before starting this recipe.
2. In a pan, add oil & sauté the onion, carrot & celery for 5 minutes.
3. Add the mushrooms, beef stock, ginger, sriracha, chicken stock, low-sodium soy sauce, garlic & water.
4. Let it come to a boil, turn the heat low and simmer for 30 minutes.
5. In a pan, add 2 tbsp of oil on medium flame. Season the steak with togarashi on both sides.
6. Cook for 3 minutes on both sides. Let it rest for 10 minutes, slice thinly.
7. Strain the broth & do not use the solids. Add to the serving bowls.
8. Add noodles, top with steak & the rest of the ingredients.
9. In a pot, add water & boil.
10. Add eggs & cook for 6 minutes, turn the heat off & immediately transfer to ice-cold water.
11. Let it rest for few minutes, peel & cut in half. Serve with ramen.
12. Serve & enjoy.

NUTRITION PER SERVINGS			
CALORIES	**PROTEIN**	**CARBS**	**FAT**
309 kcal	*30 g*	*19.1 g*	*12 g*

Miso Ramen with Beef, Mushrooms & Greens

Prep Time	Cooking Time	Servings
20 min	**30 min**	**4**

Ingredients

1-star anise
5 oz. of udon noodles
6 scallions, sliced thin
2" piece of fresh ginger, sliced into matchsticks
3½ oz. of chestnut mushrooms, sliced
2 sirloin steaks
2 tbsp of miso paste
One bunch of coriander, chopped
2 tbsp of olive oil
100g of shiitake mushrooms, cut in half
200g of baby leaf greens, sliced thinly
1 red chili, sliced thin
2 eggs, soft-boiled

Instructions

1. In a pan, add 1 liter of water. Boil & add miso. Stir & add ginger, star anise.
2. Simmer on low flame.
3. Cook noodles as per package instructions.
4. Coat the steaks in oil & season well. Add to a pan, cook for 2 to 3 minutes on one side.
5. Take it out on a plate.
6. Add the greens, mushrooms to the miso pot. Simmer for 5 minutes.
7. Sauté the scallions, chili & coriander stalks in hot oil until softened.
8. Cut the steak thinly.
9. In each serving bowl, add the noodles, broth. Top with steak & other ingredients.
10. In a pot, add water & boil.
11. Add eggs & cook for 6 minutes, turn the heat off & immediately transfer to ice-cold water.
12. Let it rest for few minutes, peel & cut in half. Serve with ramen.
13. Serve & enjoy.

NUTRITION PER SERVINGS			
CALORIES	**PROTEIN**	**CARBS**	**FAT**
312 kcal	*24 g*	*22 g*	*12 g*

Seafood Ramen with Coconut Curry

Prep Time	Cooking Time	Servings
20 min	**30 min**	**4**

Ingredients

2 tbsp of red curry paste
4 cloves garlic, minced
4 eggs, soft-boiled
1 pound of crab clusters
2 tbsp of avocado oil
1 tbsp of grated ginger
4 cups of broth
1 can of (~14 oz.) coconut milk
Salt and pepper, to taste
1 tbsp of fish sauce
6 oz. of ramen noodles
1 pound of shrimp, peeled & deveined, without tails
2 heads of baby bok choy, cut in half
Chopped cilantro & scallions, to serve

Instructions

1. In a pot, saute garlic, ginger for 2 minutes.
2. Add curry paste, cook for 1 minute.
3. Add the fish sauce, broth & coconut milk. Mix well, turn the heat to medium.
4. Add crab & bok choy. Cook for 5 minutes.
5. Cook noodles as per package instructions.
6. Add shrimps to the broth, cook for 2 to 3 minutes. Add black pepper & salt to taste.
7. Add noodles to the serving bowls, add broth on top. Serve with scallions & cilantro on top.
8. In a pot, add water & boil.
9. Add eggs & cook for 6 minutes, turn the heat off & immediately transfer to ice-cold water.
10. Let it rest for few minutes, peel & cut in half. Serve with ramen.
11. Serve & enjoy.

NUTRITION PER SERVINGS			
CALORIES	**PROTEIN**	**CARBS**	**FAT**
321 kcal	33 g	19.1 g	12 g

Homemade Tsukemen

Prep Time	Cooking Time	Servings
20 min	**25 min**	**2**

Ingredients

RAMEN NOODLES

2 portions of ramen noodles

TSUKEMEN BROTH

Half lb. of pork belly, sliced thin
2 shiitake mushrooms
2 tsp of grated ginger
2 cups of chicken stock
2 minced cloves of garlic
Half tbsp of vegetable oil
1 tsp of sesame oil
3 tbsp of low-sodium soy sauce
2 scallions
Salt & black pepper to taste
Half cup of shimeji mushrooms
2 tbsp of mirin
Half tsp of rice vinegar

TOPPINGS

Chopped scallions
2 soft-boiled eggs

Instructions

1. Sauté ginger, garlic in hot oil for 1 to 2 minutes.
2. Add pork & cook until done. Add mirin, chicken stock & low-sodium soy sauce.
3. Let it come to a boil, turn the heat low and simmer for 10 minutes.
4. Add mushrooms & scallions, boil on high flame, turn the heat low and simmer for 5 minutes.
5. Add vinegar, sesame oil, salt & pepper. Mix well & turn the heat off.
6. Cook noodles as per package instructions.
7. Drain & add to the serving bowls; add the broth on top.
8. Serve with eggs & scallions on top.
9. In a pot, add water & boil.
10. Add eggs & cook for 6 minutes, turn the heat off & immediately transfer to ice-cold water.
11. Let it rest for few minutes, peel & cut in half. Serve with ramen.
12. Serve & enjoy.

NUTRITION PER SERVINGS			
CALORIES	**PROTEIN**	**CARBS**	**FAT**
513 kcal	*15 g*	*47 g*	*30 g*

Japanese Chicken Ramen (10-minutes)

Prep Time	Cooking Time	Servings
10 min	10 min	2

Ingredients

4 portions of ramen noodle cakes
1½ cups of vegetable stock
30g packet of Instant miso soup
2 BBQ chicken breasts
1" piece of peeled ginger, cut into matchsticks
1 cup of frozen edamame
2 soft-boiled eggs
Sesame seeds & chili pepper, to serve

Instructions

1. In a pot, add the miso soup, ginger, stock & water (2 cups).
2. Place on a medium flame, let it come to a boil.
3. Add the edamame, cook for 2 minutes.
4. Cook noodles as per package instructions.
5. Slice the chicken & add to the serving bowl with noodles.
6. Add the soup on top, serve with chili & sesame seeds on top.
7. In a pot, add water & boil.
8. Add eggs & cook for 6 minutes, turn the heat off & immediately transfer to ice-cold water.
9. Let it rest for few minutes, peel & cut in half. Serve with ramen.
10. Serve & enjoy.

NUTRITION PER SERVINGS			
CALORIES	**PROTEIN**	**CARBS**	**FAT**
312 kcal	24 g	16.9 g	12 g

Ramen Soup with Spicy Chicken

Prep Time	Cooking Time	Servings
20 min	**25 min**	**2**

Ingredients

1 tbsp of sriracha
1 tbsp of brown sugar
2 peeled carrots, sliced into matchsticks
2 scallions, thinly sliced
4 cups of chicken ramen broth
2 chicken breast fillets
200g of snow peas, sliced thin
2 cups of boiling water
2 soft-boiled eggs
180g of soba noodles

Instructions

1. Let the oven preheat to 180 F.
2. In a bowl, add sugar, sriracha & chicken. Toss well.
3. Cook chicken in a pan on high flame for 2 minutes on each side.
4. Transfer to a tray, bake for 8 minutes.
5. In a pan, add water & broth on high heat. Add noodles, cook for 2 to 3 minutes.
6. Turn the heat off, add snow peas & carrots.
7. In serving bowls, add the noodles. Slice the chicken & place it on the noodles.
8. Serve with scallions on top.
9. In a pot, add water & boil.
10. Add eggs & cook for 6 minutes, turn the heat off & immediately transfer to ice-cold water.
11. Let it rest for few minutes, peel & cut in half. Serve with ramen.
12. Serve & enjoy.

NUTRITION PER SERVINGS			
CALORIES	**PROTEIN**	**CARBS**	**FAT**
354 kcal	*37 g*	*43 g*	*5 g*

Turkey Ramen recipe

Prep Time	Cooking Time	Servings
20 min	25 min	4

Ingredients

150g of diced turkey breast
300 ml of vegetable stock
1 garlic clove, crushed
Half tsp of mild chili powder
2 portions of fine egg noodles
1 tbsp of olive oil
2 chili peppers, sliced
130g of frozen sweetcorn
2 soft-boiled eggs

Instructions

1. Sauté the chili powder, garlic & turkey for 2 minutes.
2. Add peppers, stock (1 tbsp) & corn; cook for 4 minutes. Add 1 tbsp of water and cook for a few seconds.
3. In a pan, add stock with water (125 ml). Let it come to a boil, add noodles, cook for 2 minutes.
4. Add the noodles to serving bowls, add the turkey on top.
5. Pour broth & serve.
6. In a pot, add water & boil.
7. Add eggs & cook for 6 minutes, turn the heat off & immediately transfer to ice-cold water.
8. Let it rest for few minutes, peel & cut in half. Serve with ramen.
9. Serve & enjoy.

NUTRITION PER SERVINGS			
CALORIES	**PROTEIN**	**CARBS**	**FAT**
241 kcal	27 g	19.1 g	5 g

Karaka Tantan Tonkotsu

Prep Time	Cooking Time	Servings
20 min	25 min	2

Ingredients

FOR THE SOUP

Half tbsp of gochujang spicy miso paste
300 to 400ml of pork bone stock
1 bunch of ramen noodles
Half tbsp of red miso
1 tsp of lard

FOR THE PORK MINCE

1 tbsp of low-sodium soy sauce
1 garlic clove, minced
1 red chili
1 tsp of sesame oil
150g of pork mince
1 tsp of vegetable oil
To serve
2 soft-boiled eggs
Nori sheets
Red pickled ginger
Scallions, thinly sliced

Instructions

1. Simmer the pork stock on low flame.
2. Add spicy miso paste, lard & red miso to the stock. Mix well. Turn the heat off.
3. Cook noodles as per package instructions & drain.
4. In a pan, brown the meat. Add the rest of the ingredients, cook for 3 to 4 minutes.
5. In serving bowls, add the cooked noodles, add soup on top.
6. Serve with pork, with the rest of the ingredients.
7. In a pot, add water & boil.
8. Add eggs & cook for 6 minutes, turn the heat off & immediately transfer to ice-cold water.
9. Let it rest for few minutes, peel & cut in half. Serve with ramen.
10. Serve & enjoy.

NUTRITION PER SERVINGS			
CALORIES	**PROTEIN**	**CARBS**	**FAT**
313 kcal	23 g	15.2 g	12 g

Prawn Gyoza Ramen

Prep Time	Cooking Time	Servings
20 min	**20 min**	**4**

Ingredients

125g packet of long-life noodles
4 cups of chicken stock
1 tbsp of low-sodium soy sauce
10g of peeled ginger, sliced thin
8 dried shiitake mushroom, thinly sliced
300g packet of prawn gyoza
1 garlic clove, sliced thin
Half tsp of sesame oil
1 scallion, thinly sliced
1 bunch of baby pak choy, cut in half
4 soft-boiled eggs

Instructions

1. In a bowl, add mushrooms & boiling water. Let them rest for 10 minutes, drain.
2. Cut the stem off.
3. In a bowl, add the noodles & boiling water. Let them rest for 3 minutes, drain.
4. In a pan, add stock, garlic, low-sodium soy sauce, water (3 cups), and ginger & sesame oil. Let it come to a boil, turn the heat to low.
5. Add gyoza, cook for 7 minutes.
6. Add the noodles to the serving bowls. Add mushrooms, pak choy on top.
7. Add the stock on top with gyoza. Serve with egg & scallions.
8. In a pot, add water & boil.
9. Add eggs & cook for 6 minutes, turn the heat off & immediately transfer to ice-cold water.
10. Let it rest for few minutes, peel & cut in half. Serve with ramen.
11. Serve & enjoy.

NUTRITION PER SERVINGS			
CALORIES	**PROTEIN**	**CARBS**	**FAT**
321 kcal	*22 g*	*19.1 g*	*12 g*

Wagamama Ramen

Prep Time	Cooking Time	Servings
20 min	**20 min**	**4**

Ingredients

5 tbsp of low-sodium soy sauce
3 cloves of garlic, cut in half
Half tsp of chinese five-spice
1 piece of fresh ginger, sliced
⅛ tsp of chili powder
700 ml of chicken stock
1 tsp of worcestershire sauce
400g of cooked chicken breast
375g of ramen noodles
2 tsp of sesame oil

FOR THE GARNISHING

100g of baby spinach
Scallions, sliced
1 nori sheet, shredded
4 tbsp of sweetcorn
4 soft-boiled eggs

Instructions

1. In a pan, add the five-spices, water (300 ml), low-sodium soy sauce (4 tbsp), ginger, garlic, chili powder, stock & Worcestershire sauce.
2. Let it come to a boil, turn the heat low and simmer for 5 minutes.
3. Adjust seasoning now; add some sugar if necessary.
4. Cook noodles as per package instructions.
5. Cut the chicken thinly. Sauté in 2 tsp of oil until browned.
6. Add cooked noodles to the serving bowls, with meat & other ingredients on top.
7. In a pot, add water & boil.
8. Add eggs & cook for 6 minutes, turn the heat off & immediately transfer to ice-cold water.
9. Let it rest for few minutes, peel & cut in half. Serve with ramen.
10. Serve & enjoy.

NUTRITION PER SERVINGS			
CALORIES	**PROTEIN**	**CARBS**	**FAT**
422 kcal	51 g	75 g	12 g

Wagamama Yaki Udon

Prep Time	Cooking Time	Servings
20 min	**20 min**	**2**

Ingredients

2 tbsp of vegetable oil
2 eggs, whisked
1 red pepper, sliced thin
20g of noyaki chikuwa
450g of udon noodles
8 cooked & peeled prawns
2 chicken thighs, boneless & skinless
1 leek, sliced thin
Sea salt & white pepper, to taste
1 green pepper, sliced thin
1 tbsp of sesame seeds, toasted
80g of beansprouts
1 tbsp of chilli oil
40g of shiitake mushrooms, sliced
1 tbsp of pickled ginger
1 tbsp of light low-sodium soy sauce
1 tbsp of crispy fried onions

Instructions

1. Season the chicken & cook in hot oil until browned.
2. Cook noodles as per package instructions. Take them out in a bowl, add chicken, whisked eggs, prawns & noyaki chikuwa. Mix well.
3. Add oil in a wok on medium flame. Sauté the vegetables, cook for 2 to 3 minutes.
4. Add noodle mixture with low-sodium soy sauce & chili oil. Stir for 2 minutes.
5. Serve with the rest of the ingredients on top.

NUTRITION PER SERVINGS			
CALORIES	**PROTEIN**	**CARBS**	**FAT**
312 kcal	*24 g*	*21 g*	*11.1 g*

Chicken, Ramen & Vegetable Soup

Prep Time	Cooking Time	Servings
20 min	20 min	4

Ingredients

2 tbsp of low-sodium soy sauce
400g of chicken breast, cut in half diagonally
1-inch piece of fresh ginger, sliced
4 cups of chicken stock
2 cups of cauliflower florets
1 garlic clove, cut in half
200g of green beans, sliced into smaller pieces
1 carrot
2 scallions, sliced thin
270g packet of ramen noodles
2 soft-boiled eggs

Instructions

1. In a pan, add water (3 cups), ginger, low-sodium soy sauce & garlic. Let it come to a boil, turn the heat low, add chicken, and simmer for 5 minutes.
2. Turn the heat off and rest for 5-7 minutes after placing a lid on top.
3. Cut carrots into thick slices.
4. Take the chicken out on a plate, strain the stock.
5. Boil the stick on medium, add carrots & noodles. Boil for 2 minutes.
6. Add beans & cauliflower, boil for 4-5 minutes.
7. Slice the chicken thinly, serve the vegetables & noodles in bowls.
8. With soup, chicken & scallions on top.
9. In a pot, add water & boil.
10. Add eggs & cook for 6 minutes, turn the heat off & immediately transfer to ice-cold water.
11. Let it rest for few minutes, peel & cut in half. Serve with ramen.
12. Serve & enjoy.

NUTRITION PER SERVINGS			
CALORIES	PROTEIN	CARBS	FAT
414 kcal	36 g	55.2 g	3 g

Wagamama Chilli Chicken Ramen

Prep Time	Cooking Time	Servings
10 min	**20 min**	**2**

Ingredients

⅛ cup of sriracha sauce
5½ oz. of egg noodles
¼ red onion, sliced thin
500 ml of chicken stock
1 marinated chicken breast
1 fresh red chili, sliced
Half cup of beansprouts
1 scallion, chopped

Instructions

1. Cook the chicken breast in oven or in a pan.
2. Cook noodles as per package instructions.
3. Add cooked noodles to a pan, add stock & sriracha. Stir well.
4. Slice the chicken thinly, place it on top of the noodles.
5. Serve with scallions & chili pepper.

NUTRITION PER SERVINGS			
CALORIES	**PROTEIN**	**CARBS**	**FAT**
458 kcal	*47 g*	*57 g*	*5 g*

Wagamama's Pimped Up Ramen

Prep Time	Cooking Time	Servings
10 min	20 min	4

Ingredients

2 garlic cloves
4 scallions
1 tsp of worcestershire sauce
1 red chilli
3 cm knob of ginger
1.2 liters of boiling water
2 chicken breasts
20g of softened butter
1 tsp of low-sodium soy sauce
20g of miso paste
60g of spinach
360g of instant noodles
10g of corn flour
4 soft-boiled eggs
1 chicken stock cube

Instructions

1. Chop the ginger, red chili, scallions & garlic.
2. Cut the chicken into strips.
3. In a pan, add oil on medium flame. Add chicken with ginger & garlic, cook until chicken is tender.
4. Add low-sodium soy sauce & Worcestershire sauce, cook, until done.
5. Add scallions & stir.
6. Mix butter with miso paste. Add corn flour & mix.
7. In a pot, add water & boil. Add noodles & stock cube, cook for few minutes.
8. Add miso paste & simmer until it thickens.
9. Add the noodles to a bowl, add spinach on top with chicken.
10. In a pot, add water & boil.
11. Add eggs & cook for 6 minutes, turn the heat off & immediately transfer to ice-cold water.
12. Let it rest for few minutes, peel & cut in half. Serve with ramen.
13. Serve & enjoy.

NUTRITION PER SERVINGS			
CALORIES	**PROTEIN**	**CARBS**	**FAT**
309 kcal	23 g	19.1 g	12 g

Spicy Miso Shrimp Ramen

Prep Time	Cooking Time	Servings
10 min	**20 min**	**4**

Ingredients

Half tsp of toasted sesame oil
2 tbsp of white miso paste
¼ cup of white onion, sliced thin
1 tsp of grated ginger
2 tbsp of avocado oil
2 minced cloves of garlic
1-2 tbsp of chili paste
2 tbsp of or low-sodium soy sauce
4 cups of chicken broth
Half lb. of peeled & deveined shrimp
2 soft-boiled eggs
8 oz. of ramen noodles
1 head of baby bok choy halved & cut into strips

Instructions

1. In a pan, add sesame oil, avocado oil, garlic, onion & ginger. Cook for 4 minutes.
2. Add chili paste & miso, cook for 2 minutes. Add low-sodium soy sauce, broth, let it come to a bowl.
3. Turn the heat low and simmer.
4. Add bok choy & shrimps to the broth. Cook for 3 minutes.
5. Adjust seasoning with chili paste & salt.
6. In serving bowls, add the noodles. Add shrimps & bok choy.
7. Pour the broth on top, in a pot, add water & boil.
8. Add eggs & cook for 6 minutes, turn the heat off & immediately transfer to ice-cold water.
9. Let it rest for few minutes, peel & cut in half. Serve with ramen.
10. Serve & enjoy.

NUTRITION PER SERVINGS			
CALORIES	**PROTEIN**	**CARBS**	**FAT**
332 kcal	*22 g*	*21 g*	*11 g*

Pork Chop Super Ramen

Prep Time	Cooking Time	Servings
10 min	**20 min**	**4**

Ingredients

400g of ramen noodles
1 garlic clove
1 knob of ginger
5 spring onions
4 pork chops
1 red chili
bunch of coriander
2 tbsp of miso paste
1 star anise
3 tbsp of low-sodium soy sauce
2 soft-boiled eggs

Instructions

1. In a bowl, add pork chops with grated ginger, garlic, & low-sodium soy sauce. Mix well & let it marinate for 10 minutes.
2. In a pan, add olive oil. Add pork chops & sear for 4 minutes on one side.
3. Add some water to deglaze & let it reduce. Cook the chops until done.
4. Slice & set them aside.
5. In a pan, add water (600 ml). Add 2 tbsp of miso paste, with star anise, scallions & red chili. Cook for 10 minutes.
6. Cook noodles as per package instructions.
7. Add noodles to the pan, with broth & pork.
8. In a pot, add water & boil.
9. Add eggs & cook for 6 minutes, turn the heat off & immediately transfer to ice-cold water.
10. Let it rest for few minutes, peel & cut in half. Serve with ramen.
11. Serve & enjoy.

NUTRITION PER SERVINGS			
CALORIES	**PROTEIN**	**CARBS**	**FAT**
323 kcal	*24 g*	*19.5 g*	*12 g*

Ginger Basil Noodles

Prep Time	Cooking Time	Servings
10 min	**15 min**	**4**

Ingredients

2 pieces of ginger, minced
3 garlic cloves, diced
10 scallions, sliced
2 tbsp of rice wine vinegar
1 tbsp of chilli oil
Basil, a bunch, chopped
4 portions of ramen noodles (4 packets)
3 tbsp of low-sodium soy sauce
3 tbsp of sesame oil
4 soft-boiled eggs
1 tsp of sugar
1 cube of vegetable stock

Instructions

1. In a bowl, mix the sugar, chili oil, sesame oil, low-sodium soy sauce & rice wine.
2. In a wok, add some oil & sauté the scallion & ginger for 3 minutes, add garlic. Cook for 2 minutes.
3. In a pan, add water & boil. Add cube & dissolve it, then add noodles cook as per package instructions.
4. Add the drained noodles to the wok with sugar sauce & basil. Stir well.
5. Serve the noodles with a soft-boiled egg.
6. In a pot, add water & boil.
7. Add eggs & cook for 6 minutes, turn the heat off & immediately transfer to ice-cold water.
8. Let it rest for few minutes, peel & cut in half. Serve with ramen.
9. Serve & enjoy.

NUTRITION PER SERVINGS			
CALORIES	**PROTEIN**	**CARBS**	**FAT**
331 kcal	*28.9 g*	*19.1 g*	*12 g*

Drunken Noodles

Prep Time	Cooking Time	Servings
10 min	20 min	4

Ingredients

400g of flat rice noodles
2 tsp of sugar
3 garlic cloves
2 red chilies
2 tbsp of low-sodium soy sauce
1 onion
2 scallions
3 tbsp of oyster sauce
A bunch of basil
400g of chicken breast
2 tsp of fish sauce

Instructions

1. Cook noodles as per package instructions.
2. Chop the onion, garlic, basil & red chilies.
3. Slice the chicken into thin slices.
4. Add the sugar, fish sauce, low-sodium soy sauce & oyster sauce.
5. In a heated wok add some oil. Sauté the chili, garlic & onion for 1 minute.
6. Add chicken & cook for 3 minutes.
7. Add the fish sauce mixture, noodles. Stir well & add basil & scallions.
8. Serve & enjoy.

NUTRITION PER SERVINGS			
CALORIES	**PROTEIN**	**CARBS**	**FAT**
312 kcal	25.9 g	21 g	12 g

Char Siu Pork Ramen with Eggs

Prep Time	Cooking Time	Servings
10 min	**20 min**	**4**

Ingredients

1 tsp of chinese five-spice
270g packet of ramen noodles
1 egg, whisked
4 pork cutlets
¼ cup of sweet low-sodium soy sauce
1 tsp of sesame oil
2 scallions, sliced into matchsticks
Half cup of coriander leaves
1 bacon rasher, chopped
1 peeled carrot, sliced into matchsticks
150g of snow peas, sliced thin
2 soft-boiled eggs

Instructions

1. In a bowl, add pork, low-sodium soy sauce (2 tbsp), black pepper & five-spice. Coat well & set it aside.
2. Cook noodles as per package instructions.
3. Grill the pork for 3 minutes on one side, take it out on a plate. Let it rest for 5 minutes.
4. Cook bacon in a pan for 2 minutes, take it out on a plate.
5. Add the oil & cook the egg into a thin omelet. Roll & take it out on a cutting board, slice it thinly.
6. Add some oil to the pan, add noodles, bacon, snow peas, omelet & carrots with scallion & low-sodium soy sauce. Cook for 2 minutes.
7. Serve the noodles with pork & scallions.
8. In a pot, add water & boil.
9. Add eggs & cook for 6 minutes, turn the heat off & immediately transfer to ice-cold water.
10. Let it rest for few minutes, peel & cut in half. Serve with ramen.
11. Serve & enjoy.

NUTRITION PER SERVINGS			
CALORIES	**PROTEIN**	**CARBS**	**FAT**
532 kcal	*44 g*	*24 g*	*28 g*

Japanese Ramen Soup with Pork

Prep Time	Cooking Time	Servings
10 min	**20 min**	**4**

Ingredients

⅓ cup of low-sodium soy sauce
2 tsp of peanut oil
4 minced garlic cloves
¼ tsp of sesame oil
500g of pork sirloin steak
Half tsp of chinese five-spice
2 tsp of grated ginger
1 red chili, sliced
4 cups of chicken stock
180g of ramen noodles
2 tbsp of mirin seasoning
150g of snow peas, sliced thin
2 hard-boiled eggs, cut in half
200g of mushrooms, cut into fours

Instructions

1. In a dish, add garlic (half), low-sodium soy sauce (2 tbsp) & sesame oil. Mix well & add pork; coat well.
2. In a pan, add oil on medium heat. Sauté the garlic, ginger, chili & five-spice.
3. Cook for 1 to 2 minutes, add low-sodium soy sauce, water (2 cups), stock & mirin. Let it come to a boil, turn the heat low and simmer for 5 minutes.
4. Grill the pork for 2 to 3 minutes on one side. Rest for 5 minutes, then slice.
5. Cook noodles as per package instructions. Drain
6. Serve the noodles with broth, pork & egg on top.
7. In a pot, add water & boil.
8. Add eggs & cook for 6 minutes, turn the heat off & immediately transfer to ice-cold water.
9. Let it rest for few minutes, peel & cut in half. Serve with ramen.
10. Serve & enjoy.

NUTRITION PER SERVINGS			
CALORIES	**PROTEIN**	**CARBS**	**FAT**
312 kcal	*24 g*	*13 g*	*11 g*

Sapporo Miso Seafood Ramen

Prep Time	Cooking Time	Servings
10 min	1 h 20 min	3

Ingredients

2 cups of water
¼ cup of dried sardines
3 minced garlic cloves
4 tbsp of miso paste
1 tbsp of sesame oil
4 cups of chicken broth
1 tbsp of ginger minced
¼ cup of dried shrimp
Half cup of corn
Half lb. of squid tentacles
⅓ lb. of shiitake mushrooms sliced
1 tbsp of low-sodium soy sauce
3 soft-boiled eggs
3 dried seaweed
1 green onion sliced
4 dried kelp
¼ cup of bonito flakes
Half lb. of scallops
1½ tbsp of butter
3 portions of ramen noodles

Instructions

1. In a pot, add water & chicken stock. Let it come to a boil.
2. In a skillet, heat the oil, sauté ginger, garlic for 2 minutes.
3. Add shrimps, sardines, cook for 5 minutes.
4. Add mushrooms cook for 3 minutes, add to the broth.
5. Add miso paste, low-sodium soy sauce, bonito flakes & kelp. Simmer for half an hour.
6. Adjust seasoning.
7. In a skillet, melt butter, sauté scallops for 2 minutes on one side.
8. Cook noodles as per package instructions.
9. In the broth, add squid, cook for 4 minutes, turn the heat off, then add scallops.
10. In serving bowls, add noodles. Serve with broth & scallion.
11. In a pot, add water & boil.
12. Add eggs & cook for 6 minutes, turn the heat off & immediately transfer to ice-cold water.
13. Let it rest for few minutes, peel & cut in half. Serve with ramen.
14. Serve & enjoy.

NUTRITION PER SERVINGS			
CALORIES	**PROTEIN**	**CARBS**	**FAT**
542 kcal	62 g	24 g	20 g

Chilli Beef Ramen

Prep Time	Cooking Time	Servings
10 min	**20 min**	**4**

Ingredients

Vegetable oil, as needed
150g of beansprouts
250g of ramen noodles
1 liter of chicken & pork stock
1 lime, cut into fours
2 sirloin steaks
2 tbsp of teriyaki sauce
1 red chili, sliced
2 tbsp of chili sauce
Coriander, as needed
2 soft-boiled eggs
Half onion
4 scallions, sliced

Instructions

1. Cook noodles as per package instructions.
2. Season the steak & grill for 1 to 2 minutes on each side. Let it rest for 5 minutes.
3. Brush the cooked steak with teriyaki & slice it thinly.
4. Boil the stock & mix the chili sauce.
5. Serve the noodles with broth & sliced steak on top.
6. In a pot, add water & boil.
7. Add eggs & cook for 6 minutes, turn the heat off & immediately transfer to ice-cold water.
8. Let it rest for few minutes, peel & cut in half. Serve with ramen.
9. Serve & enjoy.

NUTRITION PER SERVINGS			
CALORIES	**PROTEIN**	**CARBS**	**FAT**
321 kcal	*27.3 g*	*17.1 g*	*11.0 g*

Gyoza Peanut Noodles

Prep Time	Cooking Time	Servings
10 min	**20 min**	**4**

Ingredients

3 different colors peppers
Half cup of coriander
20 vegetable gyozas
1 knob of ginger
300g of egg noodles
3 carrots
Bunch of scallions
1 tbsp of peanut butter
Vegetable oil, as needed
8 tbsp of low-sodium soy sauce
1 lime
Salt, as needed

Instructions

1. Slice all the vegetables. Add to a pan (only 3 scallions) with oil, cook until softened & charred.
2. Add the rest of the scallions to a bowl, add a pinch of salt & lime juice. Mix well.
3. In a bowl, add water (4 tbsp), peanut butter & low-sodium soy sauce. Mix well.
4. Cook noodles as per package instructions. Drain & add to the wok with all the ingredients.
5. Stir well & serve.

NUTRITION PER SERVINGS			
CALORIES	**PROTEIN**	**CARBS**	**FAT**
313 kcal	*24 g*	*16.9 g*	*12 g*

Beef, Black Bean & Cashew Pappardelle

Prep Time	Cooking Time	Servings
10 min	**20 min**	**4**

Ingredients

4 tbsp of low-sodium soy sauce
4 garlic cloves
2 tbsp of rice wine vinegar
4 scallions
350g of sirloin strips
2" knob of ginger
1 red chilli
Olive oil, as needed
75g of black pepper cashews
1 onion
1 tbsp of corn flour
150g of broccoli
2 tsp of soda bicarbonate
4 tbsp of black bean sauce
400g of pappardelle ramen

Instructions

1. In a bowl, add steak with rice wine vinegar (1 tbsp), low-sodium soy sauce (1 tbsp) & 1 grated clove of garlic. Mix well.
2. Chop the red chili, broccoli, garlic, scallion, onion & ginger.
3. In a bowl, mix rice wine vinegar (1 tbsp), water (200 ml), low-sodium soy sauce (3 tbsp), black bean sauce.
4. In a cup, mix the corn flour with 2 tbsp of water.
5. In a pan, add water & boil. Add soda & pappardelle, cook as per the pack's instructions.
6. Cook the beef in hot oil for 2 to 3 minutes, take it out on a plate.
7. Sauté the scallions for 3 minutes. Add onion, ginger, red chili & garlic; cook for 4 minutes.
8. Add broccoli & cook for 3 minutes. Add sauce, let it bubble.
9. Add corn flour mixture, cook for 2 minutes.
10. Add cooked noodles, stir well, and add cashews & beef. Stir well & serve.

NUTRITION PER SERVINGS			
CALORIES	**PROTEIN**	**CARBS**	**FAT**
334 kcal	*27 g*	*25 g*	*12 g*

Wagamama's Chili Prawns with Soba Noodles

Prep Time	Cooking Time	Servings
10 min	**20 min**	**2**

Ingredients

1 tsp of toasted sesame oil
2 tbsp of rice vinegar
150g of soba noodles
1" inch piece of peeled ginger, chopped
250g of king prawns, raw & peeled deveined
2 tsp of light brown sugar
1 tbsp of low-sodium soy sauce
1 tsp of chinese chili paste
1 tbsp of vegetable oil
Half cup of coriander leaves
2 scallions, sliced
1 chopped garlic clove

Instructions

1. Cook noodles as per package instructions. Drain & toss with sesame oil (1 tsp).
2. In a bowl, add rice vinegar (2 tbsp), low-sodium soy sauce (1 tbsp), chili paste (1 tsp) & sugar (2 tsp). Mix well.
3. Cook the prawns in hot oil with garlic, ginger & scallions. Cook for 1-2 minutes.
4. Add the sauce & stir fry for 1 minute.
5. Add noodles & toss well.
6. Serve in bowls with coriander leaves.

NUTRITION PER SERVINGS			
CALORIES	**PROTEIN**	**CARBS**	**FAT**
321 kcal	*25 g*	*18.6 g*	*11 g*

Miso Cod Ramen

Prep Time	Cooking Time	Servings
10 min	**20 min**	**2**

Ingredients

MARINADE

2 tsp of mirin
1 tbsp of sesame oil
1 tbsp of low-sodium soy sauce
1 tbsp of white miso paste
4 cod fillets, with skin, sliced into two pieces
1" piece of peeled ginger, grated

VEGETABLES & SOBA

6½ oz. of cooked soba noodles
2 tsp of low-sodium soy sauce
2 cups of chopped bok choi
3 tbsp of vegetable oil
1 tbsp of fish sauce
2¼ cups of vegetable broth
1 tsp of oyster sauce

Instructions

1. In a bowl, add all the marinade ingredients. Whisk well & add cod fillet, coat well.
2. Keep in the fridge for half an hour.
3. Add the fish in oil in a skillet and skin side down on medium flame.
4. Cook the fish for 2-3 minutes on each side until golden brown. Take it out on a plate.
5. In the wok, add 1 tbsp of oil, cook the bok choi for a few minutes.
6. Add stock with fish sauces, low-sodium soy sauce & oyster sauce. Stir well.
7. In the serving bowls, add noodles. Pour broth, top with cod & bok choi.
8. Serve with scallions.

NUTRITION PER SERVINGS			
CALORIES	**PROTEIN**	**CARBS**	**FAT**
619 kcal	*49 g*	*27 g*	*36 g*

Korean Ramen with Belly Pork

Prep Time	Cooking Time	Servings
10 min	**20 min**	**2**

Ingredients

1 tbsp of gochujang paste
100g of fresh beansprouts
1 tbsp of fish sauce
50g of kale
200g of korean pork belly
1 tbsp of chicken stock concentrate
2 scallions
2 tbsp of doengjang paste
2 soft-boiled eggs
200g of udon noodles

Instructions

1. Add the fish sauce, doengjang paste, and chicken stock & gochujang paste in a pan. Mix and add the boiling water, let it come to a boil.
2. Turn the heat low & simmer.
3. Blanch the kale for 2 minutes in hot water & then in cold water.
4. Slice the Korean belly pork, microwave for 1 to 2 minutes.
5. Slice the scallions, color-separated.
6. In a bowl, add the noodles, soak in boiling water for 5 minutes, drain.
7. Add the stock with pork belly. Serve with eggs.
8. In a pot, add water & boil.
9. Add eggs & cook for 6 minutes, turn the heat off & immediately transfer to ice-cold water.
10. Let it rest for few minutes, peel & cut in half. Serve with ramen.
11. Serve & enjoy.

NUTRITION PER SERVINGS			
CALORIES	**PROTEIN**	**CARBS**	**FAT**
977 kcal	*34 g*	*87 g*	*57 g*

Wagamama's Yasai Chilli Men

Prep Time	Cooking Time	Servings
15 min	30 min	2-3

Ingredients

CHILLI MEN SAUCE

2 lemongrass stalks, sliced
2 diced garlic cloves
1 red onion, diced
1½ tbsp of low-sodium soy sauce
2 tbsp of vegetable oil
2 to 3 tsp of grated ginger
2 tsp of chili paste
Splash of lime juice
2 tsp of sugar
1 red bell pepper, chopped
¼ cup of tomato sauce

REMAINING INGREDIENTS

7 oz. of buckwheat soba noodles
1 small zucchini, sliced
1 red bell pepper, diced
1 small red onion, sliced
1 cup of broccoli florets
2 tbsp of oil
1 scallion, sliced thin
1 cup of green beans

Instructions

1. In a pan, add oil on medium flame. Sauté the chili, lemongrass, onion, garlic & ginger until soft.
2. Add chili paste, tamari, diced pepper & sugar. Cook for 8 to 10 minutes.
3. Add water (1¼ cup), tomato sauce, simmer for 10 minutes. Pulse with a stick blender & add lime juice.
4. Cook noodles as per package instructions.
5. In a wok, add oil until smoking.
6. Add all vegetables & sauté until tender-crispy.
7. Cook noodles as per package instructions.
8. In serving bowls, add the noodles, vegetables & sauce.
9. Serve with scallions & cashews.

NUTRITION PER SERVINGS			
CALORIES	PROTEIN	CARBS	FAT
472 kcal	13 g	68 g	12 g

Chicken Yakisoba

Prep Time	Cooking Time	Servings
15 min	**30 min**	**4**

Ingredients

SOBA SAUCE

2 tsp of sugar
⅓ cup of light low-sodium soy sauce
1 tsp of dark low-sodium soy sauce
Half tsp of salt

CHICKEN YAKISOBA

3 tbsp of sunflower oil
2 eggs, whisked
1 tsp of minced ginger
2 chicken breasts, cut into thin strips
7 oz. of soba noodles
⅛ tsp of each salt, white pepper & black pepper
2 minced cloves garlic
250g of fresh beansprouts
1 red & 1 green pepper, sliced without seeds
1 onion, sliced thickly
1 tbsp of tomato ketchup
150g of cooked prawns
4 scallions, sliced
4 tbsp of hoisin sauce
⅛ tsp of chili flakes

Instructions

1. In a pan, add all the yakisoba sauce ingredients. Let it come to a boil.
2. Turn the heat low and simmer for 5 minutes.
3. Cook noodles as per package instructions.
4. In a wok, add one tbsp of oil on high flame. Cook eggs with a pinch of pepper & salt, toss & cook until scrambled. Take it out on a plate.
5. Add some oil to the wok, add chicken & cook with white, black pepper & salt. Cook for 2 to 3 minutes.
6. Add onion, garlic, peppers & ginger; cook for 2 to 3 minutes.
7. Add the rest of the ingredients, cook for 2 to 3 minutes.
8. Serve with desired toppings.

NUTRITION PER SERVINGS			
CALORIES	**PROTEIN**	**CARBS**	**FAT**
562 kcal	*42 g*	*62 g*	*18 g*

Japanese Duck Ramen Noodles

Prep Time	Cooking Time	Servings
15 min	**30 min**	**4**

Ingredients

BROTH

120g of ramen noodles
8 cups of chicken stock
Half cup of low-sodium soy sauce
10 scallions, sliced thin
2 tsp of salt
1 ginger, sliced thin
¼ cup of rice vinegar
4 duck breasts

TOPPINGS

120g of sweetcorn
300g of spinach
4 soft-boiled eggs

Instructions

1. Cook noodles as per package instructions.
2. Blanch the spinach & squeeze.
3. In a pot, add low-sodium soy sauce, chicken stock, rice vinegar, ginger & scallions. Let it come to a boil, turn the heat low and simmer for half an hour.
4. Let the oven preheat to 390 F.
5. Season the duck with salt & let it rest for 10 minutes, pat dry.
6. Bake the oven for 20 minutes. Let it rest for 15 minutes, then slice.
7. Add noodles to the serving bowls, with broth on top.
8. Add the sliced duck with the rest of the toppings. Serve.
9. In a pot, add water & boil.
10. Add eggs & cook for 6 minutes, turn the heat off & immediately transfer to ice-cold water.
11. Let it rest for few minutes, peel & cut in half. Serve with ramen.
12. Serve & enjoy.

NUTRITION PER SERVINGS			
CALORIES	**PROTEIN**	**CARBS**	**FAT**
330 kcal	*33 g*	*17 g*	*11 g*

Char Siu Pork Ramen

Prep Time	Cooking Time	Servings
15 min	**30 min**	**4**

Ingredients

2 tbsp of char siu sauce
1" piece of ginger, chopped
2 tbsp of peanut oil
600g of pork loin medallions, cut into 4 fillets
Half bunch of scallions, sliced & color-separated
180g of ramen noodles
2 garlic cloves, diced
4 cups of chicken stock
2 tbsp of low-sodium soy sauce
2 baby bok choy, cut into fours
2 tbsp of fish sauce

Instructions

1. Coat the pork in char siu sauce, let it rest for 15 minutes.
2. Saute the ginger, scallions, garlic in hot oil for 2 to 3 minutes.
3. Add water (3 cups), stock & low-sodium soy sauce. Simmer & add bok choy & noodles, cook for 3 to 4 minutes. Turn the heat off.
4. Cook pork in hot oil for 3 to 4 minutes until cooked completely. Take it out on a plate & rest for two minutes.
5. In the serving bowl, add the noodle soup with sliced pork with desired toppings.
6. Serve & enjoy.

NUTRITION PER SERVINGS			
CALORIES	**PROTEIN**	**CARBS**	**FAT**
313 kcal	25 g	21 g	13.3 g

Fish & Ramen Noodle Soup

Prep Time	Cooking Time	Servings
15 min	**30 min**	**4**

Ingredients

2 tsp of stock powder
Half tsp of sesame oil
5 cups of boiling water
1" piece of fresh ginger, cut into fours
180g of dried ramen noodles
300g of flathead fillets, sliced into 1.5"
2 tbsp of low-sodium soy sauce
3 scallions, sliced thin
1 peeled carrot, sliced into matchsticks
2 soft-boiled eggs

Instructions

1. Cook noodles as per package instructions. Drain.
2. In a pan, add water (5 cups) & stock powder, heat well & add oil, low-sodium soy sauce & ginger. Let it come to a boil.
3. Add fish, onion & carrot to the stock. Let it come to a boil, turn the heat low and simmer for 60 seconds.
4. Add noodles to the bowls, add soup & serve.
5. In a pot, add water & boil.
6. Add eggs & cook for 6 minutes, turn the heat off & immediately transfer to ice-cold water.
7. Let it rest for few minutes, peel & cut in half. Serve with ramen.
8. Serve & enjoy.

NUTRITION PER SERVINGS			
CALORIES	**PROTEIN**	**CARBS**	**FAT**
238 kcal	*22 g*	*33.3 g*	*2 g*

Easy Tantanmen Ramen

Prep Time	Cooking Time	Servings
15 min	**30 min**	**4**

Ingredients

FOR TARE

1 tbsp of chili oil
3 tbsp of tsuyu
2 tbsp of tahini

FOR MEAT

3 minced cloves garlic
1 oz. of chopped ginger
2 tbsp of chili oil
1 tbsp of chinese chili bean paste
1 tbsp of oyster sauce
Half lb. of ground pork or other meat
3 tbsp of rice wine

FOR SOUP

2 tsp of chicken powder
1 cup of water
2 cups of cashew milk

FOR NOODLES & TOPPINGS

2 portions of dried ramen noodles
2 soft-boiled eggs
1-2 green onions, sliced
1 baby bok choy, cut into fours

Instructions

1. In a bowl, add all ingredients of tare, whisk well.
2. In a pot, add chicken powder, milk & water. Turn the heat low and simmer.
3. Sauté the ginger & garlic in chili oil, for 30 seconds.
4. Add oyster sauce & toban djan, cook for 45 seconds.
5. Add pork, cook for 1 minute. Add rice wine, cook for 3-4 minutes. Turn the heat off.
6. Blanch the bok choy in salted water.
7. Cook noodles as per package instructions. Drain & add to the bowl, top with broth & the rest of the ingredients.
8. In a pot, add water & boil.Add eggs & cook for 6 minutes, turn the heat off & immediately transfer to ice-cold water.
9. Let it rest for few minutes, peel & cut in half. Serve with ramen.
10. Serve & enjoy.

NUTRITION PER SERVINGS			
CALORIES	**PROTEIN**	**CARBS**	**FAT**
662 kcal	*29.3 g*	*56 g*	*35 g*

Mushroom & Shrimp Ramen

Prep Time	Cooking Time	Servings
15 min	**30 min**	**4**

Ingredients

Kosher salt
¼ cup of low-sodium soy sauce
1 bunch of scallions, sliced thin
1 pound of shrimp, peeled & deveined
2 tbsp of sesame oil
4 minced garlic cloves
2 tbsp of minced fresh ginger
1 bunch of watercress, chopped
1 tbsp of raw sugar
12 oz. of ramen noodles
10 oz. of enoki
2 soft-boiled eggs

Instructions

1. Toss the shrimps with salt & place them in a colander; let them rest.
2. In a pot, add ginger, oil, garlic & scallions, sauté for 3 minutes.
3. Add water (6 cups), low-sodium soy sauce & sugar. Let it come to a boil, turn the heat low and simmer for 5 minutes.
4. Cook noodles as per package instructions. Drain & add to the serving bowls.
5. Wash the shrimps & add to the soup with mushrooms. Cook for 2-3 minutes.
6. Add the soup to the bowl with the rest of the ingredients.
7. In a pot, add water & boil.
8. Add eggs & cook for 6 minutes, turn the heat off & immediately transfer to ice-cold water.
9. Let it rest for few minutes, peel & cut in half. Serve with ramen.
10. Serve & enjoy.

NUTRITION PER SERVINGS			
CALORIES	**PROTEIN**	**CARBS**	**FAT**
332 kcal	*23 g*	*19.1 g*	*11 g*

Scallop Soup with Ramen Noodles

Prep Time	Cooking Time	Servings
15 min	30 min	2

Ingredients

3 oz. of ramen noodles
2½ cups of water
2 tbsp of low-sodium soy sauce
2 cups of water
5 shiitake mushrooms, sliced
2 tbsp of mirin
1 tsp of minced ginger
1 tbsp of butter
1⅓ tsp of dashi no moto
1 tsp of rice vinegar
2 green onions, sliced
8 scallops

Instructions

1. Cook noodles as per package instructions, drain & add to the soup bowls.
2. In a bowl, add water & boil. Add rice vinegar, low-sodium soy sauce, dashi & mirin. Let it come to a boil, turn the heat low and simmer for 3-5 minutes.
3. Add to the noodles.
4. Cook scallops in butter for 3 minutes & serve on top of ramen.

NUTRITION PER SERVINGS			
CALORIES	**PROTEIN**	**CARBS**	**FAT**
291 kcal	31.3 g	18.4 g	8.5 g

Chapter 5: Vegetarian & Vegan Ramen Recipes

Ramen Bowls

Prep Time	Cooking Time	Servings
15 min	20 min	2

Ingredients

1 tsp of olive oil
Half cup of shiitake mushrooms, sliced
2 minced cloves garlic
1 tsp of sesame oil
2 tsp of grated ginger
3 tbsp of low-sodium soy sauce
Half cup of shredded carrots
1 tbsp of rice vinegar
4 cups of vegetable broth
6 oz. portions of ramen
1 tbsp of sriracha sauce

Instructions

1. Sauté the ginger, garlic in hot oil for 2 to 3 minutes. Do not burn the garlic.
2. Add mushrooms & carrots, cook for 1 minute.
3. Add low-sodium soy sauce, broth, rice vinegar & sriracha sauce. Let it come to a boil, turn the heat low and simmer for 5 minutes.
4. Adjust seasonings.
5. Cook noodles as per package instructions. Drain & add to the serving bowls.
6. Add the broth to the noodles, serve with desired toppings.

NUTRITION PER SERVINGS			
CALORIES	**PROTEIN**	**CARBS**	**FAT**
581 kcal	2 g	19.1 g	7 g

Classic Miso Ramen

Prep Time	Cooking Time	Servings
15 min	**30 min**	**2**

Ingredients

3 tbsp of red miso paste
¼ cup of bean sprouts
1 tbsp of low-sodium soy sauce
1 tbsp of sesame oil
1 quart of vegetable broth
2 pieces of fermented bamboo shoots
2 garlic cloves, chopped
1 tbsp of sesame seeds, ground
2 shiitake mushroom, sliced thin
1 head of baby bok choy, cut into fours
2 scallions, sliced thin
6 oz. of ramen noodles
2 pieces of nori
1 soft-boiled egg, cut in half

Instructions

1. Heat the broth, add low-sodium soy sauce & miso. Mix well.
2. In a pan, sauté garlic for 30 seconds. Add mushrooms & cook for 5 minutes.
3. Add bok choy, bean sprouts, cook for 2 minutes.
4. Cook noodles as per package instructions. Drain & add to the bowl.
5. Add the broth with sautéed vegetables.
6. Serve with the rest of the ingredients on top.
7. In a pot, add water & boil.
8. Add egg & cook for 6 minutes, turn the heat off & immediately transfer to ice-cold water.
9. Let it rest for few minutes, peel & cut in half. Serve with ramen.
10. Serve & enjoy.

NUTRITION PER SERVINGS			
CALORIES	**PROTEIN**	**CARBS**	**FAT**
301 kcal	*13.4 g*	*12 g*	*8 g*

Ultimate Vegetarian Ramen

Prep Time	Cooking Time	Servings
15 min	**30 min**	**2**

Ingredients

¼ cup of light low-sodium soy sauce
2 tsp of honey
6 cups of vegetable stock
2 small carrots, sliced thin
2 tsp of vegetable oil
¼ cup of white miso paste
500g of skin on, kent pumpkin, sliced
thin without seeds
2 eggs, soft-boiled
2 tsp of sesame seeds, toasted
20g of dried shiitake mushrooms, sliced
2 tsp of grated ginger
1 bunch of bok choy, sliced
450g of ramen noodles
2 scallions, sliced thin

Instructions

1. Let the oven preheat to 390 F.
2. Mix the honey, oil 1 tbsp of each miso paste & low-sodium soy sauce.
3. Line a baking tray with parchment paper and brush the pumpkin with low-sodium soy sauce mixture. Roast for 15 to 20 minutes.
4. In a pan, add ginger, low-sodium soy sauce (3 tbsp), mushrooms & stock.
5. Simmer & add carrot & Bok choi, cook for 2 minutes.
6. Turn the heat off & add the miso paste; mix well.
7. Add noodles, let it rest for a minute.
8. Serve with pumpkin & soft-boiled egg.
9. In a pot, add water & boil.
10. Add eggs & cook for 6 minutes, turn the heat off & immediately transfer to ice-cold water.
11. Let it rest for few minutes, peel & cut in half. Serve with ramen.
12. Serve & enjoy.

NUTRITION PER SERVINGS			
CALORIES	**PROTEIN**	**CARBS**	**FAT**
402 kcal	19.8 g	49 g	11.9 g

Mushroom & Sesame Ramen

Prep Time	Cooking Time	Servings
15 min	**30 min**	**4**

Ingredients

250g of shiitake mushrooms, sliced
1" piece of peeled ginger, sliced
1 tbsp of low-sodium soy sauce
1 red chili, chopped without seeds
3 chopped garlic cloves
4 scallions, sliced lengthways
1 tbsp + 1 tsp of vegetable oil
250g of dried egg noodles
2 vegetable stock cubes
2 tbsp of miso paste
2 tsp of sesame seeds, toasted
1 tsp of sesame oil
250g of pak choi

Instructions

1. In a pan, add oil on high flame.
2. Add mushrooms & sauté for 4 minutes. Take it out on a plate.
3. Add some oil to the pan, sauté chili, ginger & garlic for 1 to 2 minutes. Turn the heat off.
4. In a pan, add stock, let it come to a boil. Add garlic, sesame, low-sodium soy sauce, oil, chili, miso, & ginger. Stir & turn the heat to low.
5. Cook noodles as per package instructions.
6. Add pak choi & mushrooms to the soup. Heat it well, adjust seasoning.
7. Add noodles to the bowl, top with broth & other ingredients.
8. Serve.

NUTRITION PER SERVINGS			
CALORIES	**PROTEIN**	**CARBS**	**FAT**
313 kcal	*16.9 g*	*21 g*	*11 g*

Miso Squash Ramen

Prep Time	Cooking Time	Servings
15 min	**30 min**	**4**

Ingredients

2 tbsp of toasted sesame oil
15g of dried porcini mushrooms
200g of fresh greens
1 crushed garlic clove
1 unpeeled butternut squash, cut into small chunks without seeds
5 cm piece of fresh ginger, grated
300g of cooked udon noodles
2 tsp of low-sodium soy sauce
50g of miso paste
4 eggs, soft-boiled

Instructions

1. Let the oven preheat to 460 F, toss the squash with sesame oil (1 tbsp).
2. Roast for 25 to 30 minutes.
3. Cut the greens into thin strips.
4. Sauté the ginger, garlic in hot oil for 2 minutes.
5. Add 1.7 L of boiling water with mushrooms, miso paste & sliced stalks. Simmer on a medium flame for 15 minutes.
6. In a pan, add the squash seeds, sauté for 2 minutes, add soy & cook for 1 minute; take it out on a plate.
7. Add noodles to the miso broth. Cook for 60 seconds.
8. Serve the noodles with broth, squash & desired toppings.
9. In a pot, add water & boil.
10. Add eggs & cook for 6 minutes, turn the heat off & immediately transfer to ice-cold water.
11. Let it rest for few minutes, peel & cut in half. Serve with ramen.
12. Serve & enjoy.

NUTRITION PER SERVINGS			
CALORIES	**PROTEIN**	**CARBS**	**FAT**
348 kcal	*16 g*	*47 g*	*15 g*

Marinated Tofu & Vegetable Ramen

Prep Time	Cooking Time	Servings
15 min	**30 min**	**4**

Ingredients

45 ml of low-sodium soy sauce
1 tbsp of groundnut oil
1 tbsp of honey
396g of tofu
Juice of half orange
4 oz. of soba noodles
1 red chili, sliced
3¼ oz. of bean sprouts
8 baby corn
5 oz. of mushrooms
4 baby pak choi, halved
For the ramen broth
4 liters of vegetable stock
sesame oil, as needed
4 dried shiitake
4 minced cloves of garlic
2-inches of root ginger, sliced
1-star anise
2 scallions

Instructions

1. Cut the tofu into eight slices.
2. In a bowl, mix the orange juice, low-sodium soy sauce & honey. Pour on the tofu, let it rest for 60 minutes.
3. Flip the pieces after every 15 minutes.
4. In a pan, add all the broth ingredients, let it come to a boil, turn the heat low and simmer for 10 minutes.
5. Cook noodles as per package instructions. Add to the serving bowls.
6. Sauté the tofu in oil for 1 to 2 minutes on each side.
7. In a pan, strain the broth, do not use the solids except mushrooms. Slice the mushrooms.
8. Add the corn & mushrooms to the broth, simmer for 4 minutes. Pour over the noodles.
9. Serve with the rest of the ingredients on top.

NUTRITION PER SERVINGS			
CALORIES	**PROTEIN**	**CARBS**	**FAT**
310 kcal	*15 g*	*36 g*	*10 g*

Barbecue Tofu Ramen

Prep Time	Cooking Time	Servings
15 min	**30 min**	**4**

Ingredients

396g pack of firm tofu, cut into small pieces
2 tbsp of white miso paste
3 tbsp of BBQ sauce
1½ tbsp of sesame oil
20g of mixed dried mushrooms
100g of scallions, sliced & color-separated
2 minced garlic cloves
1 tbsp of dark low-sodium soy sauce
1 lime, cut into fours
250g pack of whole wheat noodles
500 ml of oat milk
2 tsp of vegetable oil
150g of sugar snap peas
250g pak choi, halved
1 red chili

Instructions

1. In a bowl, add the mushroom, cover with boiling water. Let it rest for half an hour.
2. Toss the tofu with BBQ sauce.
3. In a pan, add sesame oil on low flame. Sauté the garlic & scallions for 2 to 3 minutes.
4. Add the low-sodium soy sauce, miso, cook for 2 minutes.
5. Add the mushrooms with liquid, mix well. Simmer for 10 minutes.
6. Add milk, low-sodium soy sauce & black pepper. Turn the heat off.
7. Sear the pak choi after tossing it with oil for 5 minutes. Take it out on a plate.
8. Add one tsp of oil to the pan, add tofu & cook for 4 to 5 minutes on one side.
9. Cook noodles as per package instructions.
10. Steam the sugar peas for 5 minutes.
11. In serving bowls, add the noodles. Pour the broth on top.
12. Add vegetables & tofu on top. Serve.

NUTRITION PER SERVINGS			
CALORIES	**PROTEIN**	**CARBS**	**FAT**
754 kcal	*35.9 g*	*111 g*	*17 g*

Vegan Ramen Noodle Soup

Prep Time	Cooking Time	Servings
15 min	**30 min**	**4**

Ingredients

1½ tbsp of minced garlic
8 cups of vegetable broth
3 tbsp of white miso
1 cup of chopped scallions
2 tbsp of dried parsley
9 oz. of ramen noodles
1 tbsp of low-sodium soy sauce
1½ tbsp of minced ginger
¾ tsp of fine salt
½ tsp of black pepper

Instructions

1. In a pan, add ginger, garlic & half a cup of broth. Simmer for 5 minutes.
2. Mix half cup of broth with miso, stir well.
3. Add the rest of the broth to the pan with miso mixture.
4. Add half a cup of scallions, parsley, pepper, low-sodium soy sauce & salt to the pot. Simmer for 5 minutes.
5. Add noodles, cook for 3 minutes. Turn the heat off & let it rest for a few minutes.
6. Serve with the rest of the ingredients.

NUTRITION PER SERVINGS			
CALORIES	**PROTEIN**	**CARBS**	**FAT**
323 kcal	*18 g*	*21 g*	*12 g*

Sesame & Tenderstem Noodles

Prep Time	Cooking Time	Servings
15 min	**20 min**	**4**

Ingredients

125g of fine egg noodles
1 tsp of clear honey
2 tbsp of low-sodium soy sauce
1 tbsp of rice wine vinegar
2 eggs, soft boiled
1 tsp of sesame seeds
1-inch piece of ginger, grated
2 sliced garlic cloves
2 tsp of toasted sesame oil
220g of tender stem broccoli, cut into smaller pieces

Instructions

1. Cook noodles as per package instructions.
2. In a bowl, whisk the low-sodium soy sauce, honey, ginger & vinegar.
3. Toss the noodles with sesame oil & add to the serving bowls.
4. Stir fry the broccoli with 3 tbsp of water for 3 minutes, add sesame oil with garlic, cook for 1 to 2 minutes.
5. Serve the noodles with broccoli & eggs on top with sesame seeds.
6. In a pot, add water & boil.
7. Add eggs & cook for 6 minutes, turn the heat off & immediately transfer to ice-cold water.
8. Let it rest for few minutes, peel & cut in half. Serve with ramen.
9. Serve & enjoy.

NUTRITION PER SERVINGS			
CALORIES	**PROTEIN**	**CARBS**	**FAT**
301 kcal	*14.9 g*	*19.8 g*	*11 g*

YakiSoba

Prep Time	Cooking Time	Servings
15 min	**30 min**	**4**

Ingredients

320g pack of vegetable mix, stir-fry
2 eggs, whisked
250g pack of dried soba noodles
2 red chilies, cut into strips without seeds
1 tbsp of olive oil
1 tbsp of toasted sesame oil
4 garlic cloves, chopped
2½-inches of ginger, grated
150g of prawns
2 tbsp of sesame seeds, toasted
3 tbsp of low-sodium soy sauce
100g of scallions, sliced

Instructions

1. Sauté the stir fry mix of vegetables for 4 to 5 minutes.
2. Cook noodles as per package instructions.
3. Add the ginger, chili & garlic to the vegetables, sauté for 2 minutes.
4. Cook the eggs for a few seconds, then add prawns and stir fry for 1-2 minutes.
5. Add the prawns, low-sodium soy sauce, noodles & sesame oil to the vegetable mixture. Stir fry well.
6. Add the sesame seeds & scallions. Toss & serve.

NUTRITION PER SERVINGS			
CALORIES	**PROTEIN**	**CARBS**	**FAT**
460 kcal	*21.4 g*	*50 g*	*17 g*

Sesame Garlic Ramen

Prep Time	Cooking Time	Servings
10 min	**10 min**	**2**

Ingredients

2 tsp of sesame oil
2 minced cloves of garlic
2 tsp of sriracha
1 tsp of brown sugar
6 oz. of ramen noodles
¼ cup of low-sodium soy sauce

Instructions

1. Cook noodles as per package instructions.
2. Sauté the garlic in hot oil for 2 minutes.
3. Turn the heat off, add sriracha, low-sodium soy sauce & brown sugar. Whisk well
4. Add the noodles, toss well & serve.

NUTRITION PER SERVINGS			
CALORIES	**PROTEIN**	**CARBS**	**FAT**
217 kcal	*17 g*	*12 g*	*12 g*

Teriyaki Tofu Miso Ramen

Prep Time	Cooking Time	Servings
10 min	10 min	2

Ingredients

2 tbsp of low-sodium soy sauce
180g of dried ramen noodles
1 red capsicum, sliced thin
125g of green beans, halved
1 tbsp of mirin
2 tbsp of white miso paste
200g of teriyaki tofu, cubed
125g of canned corn kernels, without liquid
5 cups of vegetable stock
2 scallions, sliced
100g of enoki mushrooms
2 soft-boiled eggs
2 tbsp of shredded pickled ginger

Instructions

1. In a pan, add water (2 cups), low-sodium soy sauce, stock & mirin.
2. Let it boil, add noodles, boil for 2 minutes.
3. Add beans, capsicum & cook for 2-3 minutes.
4. Take half a cup of soup out & mix with miso, add to the soup.
5. Cook for 1 minute.
6. Serve with mushrooms & tofu on top with the rest of the ingredients.
7. In a pot, add water & boil.
8. Add eggs & cook for 6 minutes, turn the heat off & immediately transfer to ice-cold water.
9. Let it rest for few minutes, peel & cut in half. Serve with ramen.
10. Serve & enjoy.

NUTRITION PER SERVINGS			
CALORIES	PROTEIN	CARBS	FAT
440 kcal	26.7 g	53 g	12.3 g

Smoky Sesame & Broccoli Ramen

Prep Time	Cooking Time	Servings
10 min	**10 min**	**2**

Ingredients

1 bunch of scallions, sliced
4 Garlic cloves
1 head of broccoli
500g of egg noodles
3 tbsp of tahini
2 red chilies
4 tbsp of dark low-sodium soy sauce
225g of smoked tofu

Instructions

1. Let the oven preheat to 390 F.
2. Only cut the broccoli stalk into smaller pieces.
3. Slice the garlic & red chili.
4. Toss the broccoli florets with crumbled tofu, oil & salt.
5. Bake for half an hour.
6. In a bowl, mix water (2 tbsp) with 3 tbsp of each tahini & low-sodium soy sauce.
7. Heat oil in a wok, sauté the stalks, scallions, red chili & broccoli stalks. Sauté for 2 minutes.
8. Add garlic, cook for half a minute.
9. Add noodles & sauce, toss well. Add tofu mixture, stir well.
10. Serve.

NUTRITION PER SERVINGS			
CALORIES	**PROTEIN**	**CARBS**	**FAT**
421 kcal	*24 g*	*21 g*	*11 g*

Vegetable Ramen with Fried Eggs

Prep Time	Cooking Time	Servings
10 min	**15 min**	**2-4**

Ingredients

10 oz. of shiitake mushrooms, sliced
6 oz. of ramen noodles
4 minced garlic cloves
2 tbsp of honey
1 cup of shredded carrots
4 scallions, sliced thin
¼ cup of low-sodium soy sauce
1 tbsp of olive oil
4 tbsp of toasted sesame oil
1½ tbsp of rice vinegar
2-4 eggs

Instructions

1. Cook noodles as per package instructions.
2. Drain all but a few tbsp of water.
3. Sauté the mushrooms in hot oil for 5 minutes.
4. Add scallions, garlic & carrots. Cook for 1-2 minutes.
5. Add vinegar, sesame oil & honey.
6. Add the drained noodles, stir well.
7. Fry the eggs in hot oil until crispy on the sides.
8. Serve with noodles on top.

NUTRITION PER SERVINGS			
CALORIES	**PROTEIN**	**CARBS**	**FAT**
320 kcal	*13 g*	*19.7 g*	*14 g*

Vegan Ramen with Charred Corn

Prep Time	Cooking Time	Servings
10 min	**20 min**	**3-4**

Ingredients

¾ oz. of kombu
4 corns on the cob
¾ oz. of peeled ginger, sliced
2 to 3 tbsp of vegetable oil
5 dried shiitake mushrooms
3 shallots, sliced
4 sliced garlic cloves
2 tbsp of white miso paste
4 tsp of chili oil
Half hot chili, sliced
1½ cup of soy milk
low-sodium soy sauce to taste
1 to 2 tbsp of rice wine vinegar
3-4 portions of dried ramen

Instructions

1. Soak the kombu & shiitake in 4 cups of water, let it rest overnight or a few hours.
2. Toss the cobs with oil & grill for 3 to 5 minutes on medium heat, all over.
3. Sauté the chili, shallots, ginger & garlic in hot oil until slightly charred.
4. Cut the kernels off the cob. Add the kernels to the shiitake & kombu with their water.
5. Simmer for half an hour.
6. Cook noodles as per package instructions.
7. Add the rest of the ingredients to the soup. Cook for a few minutes.
8. Serve with noodles.

NUTRITION PER SERVINGS			
CALORIES	**PROTEIN**	**CARBS**	**FAT**
373 kcal	44 g	13 g	17 g

Miso Corn Soup

Prep Time	Cooking Time	Servings
10 min	**15 min**	**2**

Ingredients

2 tbsp of low-sodium soy sauce
3 oz. of tender stem broccoli, stir-fried
2 to 3 tbsp of oil
7 oz. of smoked firm tofu
3 oz. of vermicelli noodles, cooked
Kernels from 2 cobs
Broth
2 diced garlic cloves
2 tsp of grated ginger
2 tsp of low-sodium soy sauce
1 tsp of toasted sesame oil
2 cups of veggie stock
1 shallot, diced
2 tbsp of rice wine vinegar
2 tbsp of white miso
1 tbsp of mirin

Instructions

1. Cube the tofu & mix with low-sodium soy sauce, let it rest for a few minutes.
2. Sauté the ginger, shallots & garlic in hot oil for 5 minutes.
3. Mix the water (2 tbsp) with miso.
4. In a pot, add stock with miso, simmer for 10 minutes.
5. Add low-sodium soy sauce, rice wine vinegar, sesame oil & mirin.
6. Cook noodles as per package instructions.
7. Sauté the tofu in hot oil until crispy.
8. Sauté the broccoli in hot oil for 2 minutes, add kernels & cook for 2 to 3 minutes.
9. In serving bowls, add the noodles.
10. Pour the soup on top, serve with desired toppings.

NUTRITION PER SERVINGS			
CALORIES	**PROTEIN**	**CARBS**	**FAT**
308 kcal	*13 g*	*22 g*	*19 g*

Vegetarian Ramen

Prep Time	Cooking Time	Servings
10 min	**35 min**	**4**

Ingredients

¼ cup + 2 tbsp of vegetable oil
1 tbsp of white or black sesame seeds
1 2-inches piece of peeled ginger, thinly sliced
1 tbsp of red pepper korean powder
1½ tsp of red pepper flakes
12 oz. of baby bok choy, cut into four lengthwise
4 garlic cloves, sliced thin
Kosher salt, to taste
4 scallions, sliced thin
2 tbsp of tomato paste
1 tbsp of soy sauce
4 packs of (5-oz.) fresh ramen noodles
12 dried shiitake mushrooms
1 piece of dried kombu, 4x3-inch piece
3 tbsp of unsalted butter, sliced into small cubes
4 eggs, nori & scallions for serving

Instructions

1. In a pot, add oil (¼ cup), add garlic & cook on medium flame.
2. Stir for three minutes, add sesame seeds & cook for one minute more until the garlic is crispy & golden. Take it out in a bowl, add the korean red pepper powder.
3. Mix well & add salt. This is your garlic chili oil.
4. Thinly slice the green & white parts of the scallions and color separate them for serving.
5. In a pan, add 2 tbsp of oil on medium-high flame. Add the white part of the scallion with ginger, stir well.
6. Cook for 4 minutes.
7. Add tomato paste & sauté for 2 minutes, until the color darkens slightly & it begins to stick to the pot.
8. Add kombu & mushrooms, mix & add five cups of water.
9. Let it come to a boil, turn the heat off. Let it rest for 10 minutes, take the kombu out & discard.
10. Add the rest of the mixture to a blender. Add 1-2 cups of broth & pulse until smooth.
11. Add in the broth & mix well. Simmer over medium heat.
12. Add butter, little by little & whisk well after adding each butter piece.
13. Add soy sauce & salt. Adjust seasoning. Turn the heat low & let it rest.
14. In a pot, add water & boil. Add bok choy & boil for 2 minutes until tender & green.
15. Take them out of the water on a plate.
16. Boil the water again & cook noodles as per package instructions.
17. Drain & add to the bowls.
18. Add the broth on top, then bok choy. Add garlic chili oil as per your taste.
19. In a pot, add water & boil.
20. Add eggs & cook for 6 minutes, turn the heat off & immediately transfer to ice-cold water.
21. Let it rest for a few minutes, peel & cut in half. Serve with ramen.

NUTRITION PER SERVINGS			
CALORIES	**PROTEIN**	**CARBS**	**FAT**
321 kcal	17 g	14 g	11 g

Vegetarian Kway Teow

Prep Time	Cooking Time	Servings
10 min	15 min	4

Ingredients

1 tbsp of vegetable oil
4 tbsp of tomato ketchup
Half of the green cabbage, sliced thin
1 onion, chopped
5 minced cloves of garlic
500g of flat rice noodles
70 ml of sweet/mild chili sauce
1 small red chili, chopped
5 scallions, cut into 1-inch pieces
4 tbsp of low-sodium soy sauce
2 tsp of sugar
200g of beansprouts
5 mushrooms - sliced
2 eggs

Instructions

1. Cook noodles as per package instructions.
2. Sauté the onion in hot oil for a few minutes. Add the sweet chili sauce, chili, ketchup, garlic, sugar & low-sodium soy sauce.
3. Stir & let it come to a boil, turn the heat low & add the scallions, mushrooms & cabbage.
4. Stir for 2 minutes.
5. Add noodles & stir well with some pasta water.
6. Add eggs after pushing noodles to one side, scramble & mix with noodles.
7. Add sprouts & cook for 2 minutes.
8. Serve with desired toppings.

NUTRITION PER SERVINGS			
CALORIES	**PROTEIN**	**CARBS**	**FAT**
759 kcal	20 g	141 g	12 g

Spicy Soy Milk Ramen

Prep Time	Cooking Time	Servings
10 min	**30 min**	**1-2**

Ingredients

FOR VEGETARIAN DASHI

1 shiitake mushroom, dried
¾ cup of water
1 piece of kombu (1 by 2-inches)

FOR SOUP

2 cloves of garlic
Half-inch of ginger
2 tsp of miso
1 cup of soy milk, unsweetened
1 scallion, sliced & use the only white part
2 tsp of sesame oil, roasted
2 tsp of spicy chili bean paste (doubanjiang)
One dash of white pepper powder
¼ tsp of kosher
1 tbsp of toasted white sesame seeds
1 tbsp of sake
2 tsp of soy sauce
Half cup of dashi

FOR RAMEN

1 portion of fresh ramen noodles

FOR RAMEN TOPPINGS

Vegetarian homemade kimchi
Ramen egg (do not use if vegan)
Scallion/green onion (green part only)
Spicy bean sprout salad
Frozen corn (or canned)

Instructions

1. In order to make dashi (vegetarian).
2. In a pot, add dried mushroom & kombu with water. Soak the ingredients for half an hour.
3. Place on a medium flame, let it come to a boil, turn the heat low and simmer for a few minutes.
4. Take the shiitake mushroom & kombu out. Turn the heat off & set it aside.
5. In order to make the soup, grind the sesame seeds roughly.
6. Mince the garlic & ginger.
7. Slice the scallions & color separate them.
8. In a pan, add sesame oil on medium flame. Add the white scallions with ginger, garlic, sauté on medium-low flame.
9. Add miso & spicy chili bean sauce in a pan. Mix well & keep stirring.
10. Add sake, & deglaze the pan with a wooden spoon.
11. Add soy sauce & roughly ground sesame seeds.
12. Add soy milk slowly to stir the miso & spicy chili bean paste. Add mushroom dashi & kombu.
13. Add salt & white pepper powder. Mix well & turn the flame off. Set it aside.
14. Now is the time to cook ramen, Cook noodles as per package instructions, but make sure not to overcook the noodles.
15. Drain all but a few tablespoons of water. Reheat the rest of the ingredients.
16. Add the noodles to a serving bowl, add the soup on top.
17. In a pot, add water & boil.
18. Add eggs & cook for 6 minutes, turn the heat off & immediately transfer to ice-cold water.
19. Let it rest for a few minutes, peel & cut in half.
20. Serve with ramen.

NUTRITION PER SERVINGS			
CALORIES	**PROTEIN**	**CARBS**	**FAT**
549 kcal	*14 g*	*63 g*	*27 g*

Vegan Ramen with Miso Shiitake Broth

Prep Time	Cooking Time	Servings
10 min	**40 min**	**4**

Ingredients

DELICIOUS VEGAN BROTH

2 minced garlic cloves
1 to 2 tbsp of olive oil
4 cups of vegetable stock
1 onion, chopped
1 sheet of kombu seaweed, it is optional
⅛ cup of mirin (cooking wine)
4 cups of water
Half cup of dried shiitake mushrooms, cut into smaller pieces
hot chili oil or sriracha, to taste
1 to 2 tbsp of white miso paste
Black pepper, to taste

RAMEN

8 oz. of crispy tofu, cut into cubes
Chili oil, sesame oil & scallions
Steamed or sautéed mixed vegetables
6 to 8 oz. of ramen noodles
Eggs, as needed

Instructions

1. Toss the vegetables with oil, salt & pepper.
2. Roast them in the oven on a parchment-lined baking sheet at 400 F, till tender-crisp.
3. To make the broth, sauté the chopped onion in 1 tbsp of hot oil for 3 minutes on medium flame.
4. Add garlic & cook until the onion is golden brown.
5. Add the whole sheet of kombu, vegetable stock, dried mushrooms, mirin & water.
6. Stir well & let it come to a boil; turn the heat low and simmer for half an hour.
7. Take the kombu out.
8. Add the black pepper & miso, stir well.
9. Add salt to your taste, add miso, soy sauce or more water. Cook on low flame to keep warm.
10. In a pot, add water & boil, cook noodles as per package instructions.
11. Drain & mix with sesame oil.
12. Steam the greens if using until slightly wilted.
13. In serving bowls, add the cooked ramen. Top with the broth.
14. Add desired vegetables on top.
15. Optional: In a pot, add water & boil.
16. Add eggs & cook for 6 minutes, turn the heat off & immediately transfer to ice-cold water.
17. Let it rest for a few minutes, peel & cut in half.
18. Serve with ramen.

NUTRITION PER SERVINGS			
CALORIES	**PROTEIN**	**CARBS**	**FAT**
408 kcal	*13.9 g*	*59.5 g*	*13.8 g*

Vegan Shoyu Ramen

Prep Time	Cooking Time	Servings
10 min	**40 min**	**2**

Ingredients

For Broth
3 minced garlic cloves
1 tbsp of sake
1 tsp of dark soy sauce, optional
1" of grated ginger
5 cups of vegetable broth
1 tbsp of sesame oil
1 sheet of kombu, cut into smaller pieces
2 tsp of sugar
4 dried shiitake mushrooms
Salt, to taste
2 to 3 tbsp of soy sauce, to taste
"Char Siu" Mushrooms
1 tsp of sesame oil
Half tbsp of sake/mirin
1 tbsp of soy sauce
150g of fresh mushrooms
2½ tbsp of brown sugar
Noodles
2 portions of fresh ramen noodles
Toppings
Chilli oil
Vegan "fish" cakes, cut into thin slices
Sesame seeds
Chopped scallions
Nori sheets, cut into smaller pieces

Instructions

1. To make the broth: add sesame oil to a pan on medium flame.
2. Add the ginger, garlic & sauté for 1 to 2 minutes.
3. Add kombu, vegetable broth & dried mushrooms. Mix & add sugar, sake & soy sauce.
4. Heat the broth for 5 to 8 minutes on medium flame.
5. Let it come to a boil, turn the heat low and simmer for 20 minutes.
6. Adjust seasoning & add more salt & soy sauce.
7. Take the mushrooms & kombu out. Cool for a few minutes, then thinly slice.
8. To make the char siu mushrooms.
9. In a pan, add the sesame oil, sugar, mirin & soy sauce on medium flame.
10. Keep whisking till the sugar dissolves.
11. Add the mushrooms, coat the mushrooms well.
12. Let them cook for 4 to 5 minutes. Do not let the mushrooms burn. Keep an eye on the mushrooms. Turn the heat off once they get golden brown.
13. Cook noodles as per package instructions.
14. Add the cooked noodles to the two serving bowls.
15. Add the toppings on top & serve.

NUTRITION PER SERVINGS			
CALORIES	**PROTEIN**	**CARBS**	**FAT**
505 kcal	*6 g*	*57 g*	*10 g*

Tonkotsu Style Veg Ramen

Prep Time	Cooking Time	Servings
10 min	**30 min**	**4**

Ingredients

Chili Garlic Oil
1 tbsp of white & black sesame seeds
¼ cup of vegetable oil
Half tsp of salt
4 cloves of garlic, sliced
1 tbsp of red chili flakes
Ramen Broth
8 dried shiitake mushrooms
4 scallions, sliced, color-separated
2-inches of ginger peeled & sliced
1 tsp of sesame oil
2 tbsp of vegetable oil
2 tbsp of tomato paste
6 cups of water
1 tbsp of soy sauce
Vegetables
2 tbsp of chives, chopped
1 cup of matchsticks carrot
1 to 2 cups of cooked noodles
4 to 6 bok choy
1 cup of sliced mushrooms

Instructions

1. In a pan, add oil & heat on medium flame.
2. Add garlic & sauté for 1 minute. Add sesame seeds, cook for 30-60 seconds more.
3. Turn the heat off & add to a bowl. Add salt & chili flakes, stir well.
4. In a pot, add 2 tbsp of oil. Sauté the ginger for 2 to 3 minutes.
5. Add the scallions & cook until lightly charred.
6. Add tomato paste & sauté for 1 to 2 minutes.
7. Add some water & boil. Turn the heat low and simmer for 10 minutes. Strain & turn the heat off.
8. Add salt, soy sauce & sesame oil.
9. Saute the bok choy until tender-crisp.
10. In the serving bowl, add the noodles & other vegetables.
11. Add broth. Serve with scallions & chili oil on top.

NUTRITION PER SERVINGS			
CALORIES	**PROTEIN**	**CARBS**	**FAT**
660 kcal	40 g	84 g	28 g

Japanese-Inspired Ramen Noodle Soup

Prep Time	Cooking Time	Servings
10 min	**30 min**	**2**

Ingredients

2 tbsp of sesame oil
1 ginger knob
2 garlic cloves
1 tsp of black sesame seeds
2 tbsp of soy sauce
Red chili
1 carrot
A few florets of broccoli
5 oz. of noodles dried
1 cup of shredded red cabbage
1 courgette
2 baby bok choy
4 cups vegetable stock
3 scallions
1 cup of shiitake mushrooms
1 lime

Instructions

1. Saute the ginger, garlic in hot oil with soy sauce.
2. Add the vegetables & stir well. Add a splash of water.
3. Place a lid on top, let it steam for 2 to 3 minutes until tender to your liking.
4. Heat the stock & season with soy sauce or salt.
5. Cook noodles as per package instructions.
6. In a bowl, add the cooked noodles, add the broth on top.
7. Serve with steamed vegetables & a drizzle of chili oil.

NUTRITION PER SERVINGS

CALORIES	PROTEIN	CARBS	FAT
596 kcal	*23 g*	*83 g*	*21 g*

Vegan Ramen with Mushrooms

Prep Time	Cooking Time	Servings
10 min	**10 min**	**2**

Ingredients

2 cups of chopped mushrooms
4 oz. of ramen noodles
1½ tbsp of soy sauce
2 tsp of vegetable oil

FOR THE SOUP

1 tsp of vinegar white
2 tsp of sweet chili dipping sauce
2 cups of vegetable stock
1 tsp of soy sauce
Pinch of sugar

Instructions

1. Sauté the mushrooms in hot oil for 2 minutes.
2. Add soy sauce cook for 2 minutes.
3. Cook noodles as per package instructions.
4. In a pot, add all ingredients of broth. Cook on low flame until it boils. Turn the heat off.
5. In serving bowls, add noodles top with broth & desired toppings.

NUTRITION PER SERVINGS			
CALORIES	**PROTEIN**	**CARBS**	**FAT**
335 kcal	*2 g*	*45 g*	*13 g*

Tantanmen Ramen

Prep Time	Cooking Time	Servings
10 min	**30 min**	**4**

Ingredients

FOR THE TARE

1 tsp of sugar
70g of tahini
30 ml of chili oil
40 ml of light soy sauce
For The Tofu
1 clove of garlic
1 tsp of light soy sauce
1-inch knob of ginger
220g of firm tofu
1 tsp of chilli oil
2 tsp of dark soy sauce
1 tsp of mirin

FOR THE BROTH

2 tsp of light soy sauce
250 ml of soy milk
340g of ramen noodles
2 tbsp of miso paste
4 heads of pak choi
2 scallions

Instructions

1. In a bowl, add all tare ingredient mix & set it aside.
2. Sauté the crumbled tofu in hot oil for 3 minutes. Add ginger, garlic, cook for 1 minute.
3. Add the rest of the ingredients, cook until combined.
4. Cut the vegetables.
5. In a pan, add soy sauce, water (1.5 liters) & soy milk. Simmer & add miso.
6. Add noodles & pak choi cook for 3 minutes.
7. In the serving bowl, add tare & broth with noodles & vegetables.
8. Serve.

NUTRITION PER SERVINGS			
CALORIES	**PROTEIN**	**CARBS**	**FAT**
309 kcal	*13 g*	*11 g*	*7 g*

Conclusion

Ramen is affordable and readily accessible, making it an excellent choice for budget visitors. Ramen restaurants, also known as ramen-ya, may be found in almost every part of Japan, serving a variety of regional variants on the popular noodle dish. The ideal places to consume ramen are specialist ramen restaurants, such as the abovementioned ramen-ya, which can be located in crowded areas like railway stations, amusement districts, and busy roadways. Ramen-ya is typically a sit-down restaurant featuring a counter and a few tables. However, smaller establishments may just have one. Some ramen-ya only have standing counter space in popular areas.

Ramen is also often seen on the menu of other eateries that provide an enormous variety of meals, such as tourist restaurants, izakaya, local restaurants, and food vendors. Hot ramen meals are also available 24 hours a day in convenience shops and vending machines.

In Japan, ramen isn't the only thing to eat. Ramen has undoubtedly captured the hearts (and tummies) of people all around the globe, but it now comes in a variety of forms. A restaurant, for example, in New York that combines contemporary and traditional design elements. While the furnishings are primarily gloomy and austere, stylish geometric patterns and light pink tones provide fresh vitality to the area.

However, several eateries try to reproduce the real ramen experience in other regions of Asia. Another popular eatery is in the Philippines, and it emulates many traditional elements of ramen restaurants, such as its small sitting capacity and the restricted menu of just 3 options. The most incredible method to advertise ramen worldwide, much as in Japan, is to get the ingredients correctly. They're also more frequently than not managed by Japanese ramen cooks, rather than businesses wanting to cash in on this creamy bowl. But, worry not. This book will guide you on how to build your first bowl of authentic ramen.

Thank you so much for reading it to the end of this book. Most people who appreciate the taste of this distinctive part of Asian food are now learning to cook it at home. In order to produce ramen at home, you don't have to be a top-class cook. The first few attempts might not end up as successful as you planned. All it takes is a little practice and you'll be able to get great ramen dishes at home.

If you enjoyed this cookbook, please leave me a short review on Amazon with a picture of your first recipe!

Thank you ☺

Made in the USA
Coppell, TX
29 September 2023

22179811R00063